AMERICAN IDENTITY IN CRISIS

AMERICAN IDENTITY IN CRISIS

Notes from an Accidental Activist

Kat Calvin

AMISTAD

An Imprint of HarperCollins*Publishers*

The names and identifying characteristics of some of the individuals featured throughout this book have been changed to protect their privacy.

HarperCollins books may be purchased for educational, business, or sales promotional use. For information, please email the Special Markets Department at SPsales@harpercollins.com.

FIRST EDITION

Designed by Michele Cameron

Library of Congress Cataloging-in-Publication Data
Names: Calvin, Kat, author.
Title: American identity in crisis : notes from an accidental activist / Kat Calvin.
Description: First edition. | New York : Amistad, HarperCollins, [2023]
Identifiers: LCCN 2023016236 (print) | LCCN 2023016237 (ebook) | ISBN 9780063273160 (hardcover) | ISBN 9780063341920 (trade paperback) | ISBN 9780063273177 (ebook)
Subjects: LCSH: Voting—United States. | Suffrage—United States—History. | Political participation—United States. | Democracy—United States. | United States—Politics and government—History.
Classification: LCC JK1967 .C22 2023 (print) | LCC JK1967 (ebook) | DDC 324.6/20973—dc23/eng/20230613
LC record available at https://lccn.loc.gov/2023016236
LC ebook record available at https://lccn.loc.gov/2023016237

ISBN 978-0-06-327316-0

23 24 25 26 27 LBC 5 4 3 2 1

To Gina, Emma, Marissa, Jennifer, Adam,
Ms. Kat, Patsy, Lou, Chris B., Chris de R.,
My'Easha, Aisha, Carol, and Sean.
We built this together.

To Mom, for teaching me about Marion,
Gloria, Mary, and the hundreds of other women
who have changed the world.

To my grandmother, Dorothy Coston Tompkins, for
being the target my arrow is always pointing toward.

Let us go forth to lead the land we love.

—John F. Kennedy, Inaugural Address,
January 20, 1961

Contents

CONTENTS

Introduction

You cannot buy the revolution. You cannot make
the revolution. You can only be the revolution.
It is in your spirit, or it is nowhere.

—Ursula K. Le Guin, *The Dispossessed*

I had always wanted to experience Armageddon at the Cosmo-politan. My favorite Vegas resort has the combination of James Bond–themed bars, José Andrés restaurants, and free drinks on the casino floor that I thought would give my apocalypse the overstated dramatic flair that it deserved. So, when I found my-self at a bar at the Cosmopolitan on election night in 2016, I was surprised to find that it wasn't as fun as I had imagined—fewer zombies, more shock, and deep, dark depression.

After a day of working election protection, I was in need of a drink and a win.

I'd arrived at the polling place in one of the calm, cozy Las Vegas neighborhoods that no one knows exists, with two other lawyers, both white, to find an elderly white woman sitting in the roped-off area, approximately the size of an airplane bathroom. She wouldn't tell us which campaign she was with but made a point to shake the two white lawyer's hands and not mine. As my hand sat there, in the air, naked, alone, unshaken, I had a feeling that this was going to be a very long day.

The old lady, whose paperwork had "**TRUMP**" written on it so loudly that I'm not sure how she thought we would miss it, called in reinforcements, and for the rest of the day we tried to protect an election from angry white people who ostentatiously wrote down the license plate of every car driven by a brown person, screamed "Voter fraud!" every time we spoke to a voter a hundred yards away from the polling place, and called the police on a Black woman who was walking seniors over from the nearby nursing home.

All day we kept saying to one another, "It's okay. They're going to lose. It's okay." We did our best to make people feel safe and reported every incident on the Democratic Party's less-than-perfect, but perfectly named, voter protection reporting program, LBJ. When I did voter protection in Ohio in 2008, I was at a mostly Black polling place in Dayton, and when I arrived at 5:00 a.m. on Election Day, there was already a celebratory line. Despite the police car that stayed parked close to the polling place and the occasional person turned away for one reason or another, the day was celebratory, peaceful, joyful.

It was different in every way from the painful, humiliating, dangerous-feeling Election Day in Las Vegas.

At the end of the night, our team stayed to help clean up; thankfully, the Trump "voter protection" team left as early as possible. I was put in charge of watching the polls. I kept refreshing the *New York Times* needle and saying, "Umm . . . something is wrong here."

Something is not going right. Something is not right. We decided to skip the party and go to a bar. My bar.

The Cosmopolitan has a bar in the middle of the casino floor with a beautiful chandelier. Vesper. I love it there. But that night I stared at the crystals to avoid looking at the TV.

I went to bed that night knowing I had no choice.

After law school I started a nonprofit, and a social enterprise, and a social group for young entrepreneurs. I ran them all while doing occasional legal work for money for my student loans and rent and pie. Unsurprisingly, I crashed, right around the time that I was finally diagnosed with a chronic illness. I had been trying to convince doctors that something was wrong with me since I was twelve, but what did I know? I was just a Black woman with a body. I quickly got a terrible job with good health insurance, suffered through it for a year, and then left the capital city I adored for warmer climes. As I arrived in Los Angeles, I swore that I would never start another nonprofit. That vow lasted a year, almost to the day.

My retirement was over. It was time to jump back in.

Every Angeleno knows that a drive to and from Vegas will solve almost any problem. On the way home, I made a plan. There was one issue that I had been mildly obsessed with, an issue that no one except the wonderful journalist Ari Berman and a few voting rights groups had been talking about. An issue that could have changed the 2016 election: voter ID laws. That, I decided, would be my new mission.

On December 20, I pushed "send" on a tweet that would change my life: "If anyone is interested in working on a project to help people get state IDs so they can vote, DM me."

"I'm so frustrated and want to do something. How can I help?"

"I'm a lawyer too—can I help with research?"

"I have no skills, but I'm super enthusiastic!"

I spent two weeks sneaking out of my office to talk to potential volunteers and put together a team. Soon I had about twenty people ready to help.

Within weeks, Spread The Vote was born.

1

Doesn't Everybody Have an ID?

*Anyone who has ever struggled with poverty knows
how extremely expensive it is to be poor.*

—James Baldwin, "Fifth Avenue, Uptown"

My first-ever ID client was Ms. Ella. She was born in either 1942 or 1947 and had lived in Georgia all of her life. I had been trying to find someone to trust us enough to let us help them get their ID when a partner organization in Atlanta called. Gary, a man I would soon get to know well, had called and asked if someone could help his family friend Ms. Ella get an ID. She was ailing, suffering from four types of cancer at the same time, and she needed an ID to get better medical care. Gary had known Ms. Ella his entire life, and she had helped him nurse his father through liver cancer, so now he was returning the favor. But Ms. Ella didn't have any documents, wasn't sure of her real birth date, and didn't think she'd ever even had a birth certificate, so Gary had no idea where to turn. I jumped on this case with extreme fervor. I really wanted to get our first ID, but it was also immediately clear that Ms. Ella's life depended on it. If I met Ms. Ella now, it would still be a real challenge, but we would be able to help her. We know so much more now than we did back then about getting IDs. At the time, my small team and I did everything we could. A volunteer went to Ms. Ella's house in rural Georgia and found old insurance policies and newspaper clippings that we might have been able to use as proof of life for a delayed birth certificate. Incredibly, her elementary school still had her transcripts. In some states, you can use a birth record in a family Bible as a birth certificate substitute, but only if the preacher who wrote the record was still alive to sign an affidavit. Ms. Ella's childhood minister most certainly was not. We didn't know then that we could submit a Freedom of Information Act request to the Social Security Administration for an obscure document called a Numident record to confirm her birth.

We know that now, but even after we figured out how to make the request in a way that the SSA would accept, it still takes months to hear back.

After a while, with no success finding a suitable birth document and with Ms. Ella's health declining every day, we decided to try for a passport. Theoretically, with enough proof-of-life documents, you can get a passport without a birth certificate. Getting a passport is tough in a different way than getting a Department of Motor Vehicles ID is tough, and getting a passport is much more expensive, but it was worth a shot. It took more than one try to get Ms. Ella to the post office to apply for her passport because she kept having medical emergencies. Eventually we got her there, applied with a mountain of documents that the passport employee thought—but wasn't sure—would work, and waited. And waited. And waited. And then: rejection. Devastated, we read the reasoning (none of the documents were acceptable as proof of citizenship) and decided to try again. As we were trying to find more documents, Ms. Ella's sister called. She had found Ms. Ella's birth certificate! I almost shrieked with joy. I arranged to meet with Gary and Ms. Ella to take her to the DMV. On my way, he called: Ms. Ella had been rushed to the hospital. She couldn't make it to the DMV. It turned out that she never would. She died a few days later, more than a year after we started her ID journey. My first client would also be the one who never got an ID.

I think about Ms. Ella every day. She is the reason that we must make it easier to get an ID. She is the reason I do what I do.

I was a normal sixteen-year-old. Okay, that's not true. I was a nerd. At sixteen, I absolutely lived for Kenneth Branagh's Shakespeare remakes and Advanced Placement homework. But in one way I was very, very normal: I couldn't wait to drive.

I already had plenty of government-issued ID. I'd had a passport since I was an infant. I got my military ID when I was ten. I had never known a waking moment without ID. But I didn't have a driver's license yet. As the only student in my class who was a year younger than the others, this was a particular torture.

All of the other kids were zipping around town, leaving campus for lunch, and showing up to dance team on their own recognizance, while I was reduced to *asking for rides*. Humiliating. Now, unlike the other kids at my overly privileged public school, there was no way my single mother was going to be able to afford to buy me a car, so this ride thing was going to last for quite a while; but I had deluded myself into thinking that if I got a license, a car would just magically show up.

My public school, like many before it and many, many after, had stopped offering driver's ed who knows how many years before. There was a private driving school down the road, and although my mother didn't have a lot of extra cash, she also desperately wanted me to pick up groceries and ferry my brother around. So she came up with the money, and I signed up for driver's ed. I watched the boring videos; I sat on a pillow in the ancient Crown Vic practice car; I studied harder for my driver's test than for the SAT, for which I had been practicing since the sixth grade. Finally, finally, the day came. I did all the things. I parallel parked the car. I turned on the left-turn signal. I took the written test. I got my license. Bliss. Unsurprisingly, a car did not appear, but just *having a driver's license* made me feel like an adult. And in the more than twenty years since then, I have never had to go a day without one.

This is a typical American story, and most of us think that this is everyone's story. After all, how hard is it to find money for driver's ed, and someone to drive you to lessons and home again, and someone to give you a car to take the test with, and someone who has been holding on to your birth certificate for six-teen years even though you've moved nine times because you're an Army brat, and someone who can also figure out all of the other types of documents you need to get an ID even though you don't own anything and don't pay bills and have nothing in your name? And then that person has to be willing to pay for your license and insurance—or you have to have an ID to get a job to pay for insurance on your own, and then you can't make any mistakes (or be wrongly accused of making mistakes) that might get your license taken away and have fines and fees put on it, and you have to do that for the rest of your life and also be extremely lucky and never have a hurricane sweep your house away or a fire burn it down or be evicted because medical bills bankrupted you or you lost your job during a global pandemic, so now you're living on the street, and your license and documents have been lost / stolen / confiscated / set on fire by the police. If you are one of those very, very lucky people, congratulations; please go buy a lottery ticket right now.

Most people with a driver's license in their wallet right now remember the process as a pretty easy one, even if it wasn't easy at the time. We forget the long hours at the DMV and the document search; we just know that we have an ID and here it is and we did it, so it must be a thing that can be done. And we are in such a wildly wealthy and privileged country—for most of us, anyway.

Well . . . more or less.

Just while writing this book, I have personally dealt with the DMV three times (I have visited the DMV with clients literally hundreds of times, but this is the life I've chosen). First, I renewed my license online. Easy-peasy. I just needed, you know, money and an internet connection—two things that the vast majority of Spread The Vote clients do not have. Then I decided I may as well get a REAL ID; I run an ID organization, so maybe I should have the latest and greatest form of ID. For this, I had to find my birth certificate and two proofs of residency. I am fortunate to somehow still have my original birth certificate, and I pay utilities and have a bank account (unlike sixty-three million unbanked Americans), so I could easily print those documents. And by "easily" I mean I could save them as a pdf, email them to FedEx, drive to FedEx, and print them.

Next, I had to *go to the DMV*. I got there an hour before it opened. The line was around the building. I waited for more than an hour before I found out that there was a secret, smaller line for those of us who had uploaded all of our documents online and made an appointment. Everyone missed this line, because the sign was apparently designed for elves. So then I waited in *that* line for thirty minutes until I finally got the privilege of waiting inside for an hour before presenting an absurd number of documents and getting my REAL ID. After taking a hideous new picture. And waiting up to sixty business days. And having it mailed to my apartment with a reliable mailbox, which I am very lucky to have.

Success!

Then, like a true moron, I had to go back to the DMV mere weeks later, because I decided it would be really fun to have a motorcycle license (it is). And so yet again, I arrived more than an hour before the DMV opened. Once again, the line was around the building. This time, I wasn't able to make an appointment so I had to wait in the plebeian line for longer than a hobbit's lifetime, just to get inside and wait for honestly so long I think I blacked out. And *then* after presenting all of my documents again (as a person who had received not one but *two* valid IDs in the past two months), I had to take an eye test (a daunting task for a nerd who has worn glasses since she was seven), take yet another hideous photograph, wait in line for another thirty minutes to take a written exam, and then WAIT IN ANOTHER LINE FOR ANOTHER THIRTY MINUTES to present yet more documents, before finally receiving a little piece of paper informing me that I would be getting yet another ID in the mail in up to sixty business days. And this was an *optimal* DMV experience. I am a person with nothing but time on my hands, who has more identifying documents than some presidential candidates, and who runs an entire organization that does nothing but help people get IDs. Oh, and I always had a valid ID each time I went to the DMV to just basically get an upgrade. I defy you to find a single person in this country for whom getting an ID is easier. But for more than twenty-six million adults in America, to do what I did is next to impossible. Assembling the pile of required documents ranges from difficult but doable in some states to resembling the extraction of "a pound of flesh without drawing blood" in others. Now that you've seen the easiest possible way to get an ID, let's hop on the opposite of the Magic School Bus and take a more detailed journey into the process of getting an ID.

• • •

First stop: You have to prove your identity. This is usually done with a birth certificate, which 57 percent of our clients don't have. Take a second and think about where your birth certificate is. Do you know? If so, congratulations, you are one of the very few people who can immediately pull it up. For most people who have homes and stability, finding their birth certificate is still a wild ride. Now try being someone who has moved a lot or was evacuated because of a hurricane or wildfires. Or perhaps you're like one of our clients, whose mother always kept her documents; but then her mother passed away, and our client's aunt immediately threw away everything the mother owned—including our client's birth certificate. The day you're born you're good at two things: pooping and crying—I think. I don't know a lot about babies, so maybe they don't poop on day one. If so, then all you're good at is crying. Maybe eating? Do they sleep? This is not a book about babies. The point is, one thing that I know babies for sure are not good at is holding on to documents.

So let's say that you're one of those unorganized babies who can't keep a few pieces of paper together, and now thirty-four years later you need an ID. And for that you need a birth certificate. If you go to Vital Records and ask for a birth certificate, they'll ask for your ID. So what next? Well, there's a little website, VitalChek, which we'll talk about in chapter 3, that is a lifesaver but also one of the most absurdly challenging ways to prove your identity short of literally chopping off a finger and putting it in the mail. It's also expensive. It costs us thirty to ninety dollars to get a birth certificate this way. And don't be a naturalized citizen who needs a new Certificate of Naturalization. Those puppies cost as much as one pair of Chloé flats or sixty-nine reasonably priced burritos—$555— for a document the government can literally print out at any second. And perhaps you were born in Puerto Rico and need a new birth certificate from our should-be-fifty-second state (after Washington, DC). Well, first of all, PR recently invalidated all birth certificates before July 1, 2010, so, yes, you do need a new one. Second, until very recently you needed everything to be done in person in PR. After Hurricane Maria, we had to have a street team in Puerto Rico running around getting documents notarized and signed for the many evacuees we were helping in Orlando. So hopefully you have someone at home. And what if you were born in a country where perhaps the administrative services are not as "easily" navigable as in some other places? It's an adventure. You can't just walk into the DMV and prove that you were, in fact, born because you are, in fact, standing there. You need a piece of paper to prove it. But let's say you've done that. Hurrah! You have a birth certificate. You've accomplished step one.

Next step: You have to prove that you have a Social Security number. In most states, this means having an actual physical Social Security card, or maybe a W-2 or tax return, which you are unlikely to have if you are unhoused or unemployed or a returning citizen or . . . [enter demographic here]. So you need a card. You guys, let me tell you, getting a Social Security card without an ID would be comical if it wasn't so serious. It is easier to hitch a ride on Richard Branson's space plane than to get someone a Social Security card without an ID. We once managed to get a card for someone only because our volunteer cried. I'm not kidding. We had piles of documentation; spent months trying to prove that our client was a human being with a Social Security number; and finally, on like the third visit to the Social Security office, our volunteer broke down and cried. And I swear on Thor's abs, within minutes, the agent pulled up the client's number and printed up a card—because of course the agents can do that. Over the years we have found many more ways to get a Social Security card, the easiest being to visit a medical facility, get an exam, and then ask for a very specific piece of paper to then mail to the SSA. Again, not kidding. So okay, you either cried or saw a doctor about a headache, and the SSA miraculously gave you a nice, shiny, new *paper card* that you are supposed to hold on to for the rest of your life (there is a lifetime limit of ten). Now you have accomplished step two.

On to step three (I know—I can't believe we're not done yet, either). You've proven that you were born and that you had a number randomly assigned to you at said birth. Now you have to prove that you are a person who lives somewhere—which is especially difficult if you are a person who does not live anywhere. But let's say you do live somewhere. Congrats! You're one of the fortunate ones. Now go find your mortgage or lease, or a utility bill, or a bank statement (you too will probably have to get some of these printed out, which means a trip to FedEx or your mom's house, because who owns a printer?), government-issued correspondence (whatever that is), your voter registration card, or your concealed weapons permit—or maybe just bring along a copy of the taxes you filed last year. Oh, by the way, you'll probably need two of these documents—maybe three or four—if you want a REAL ID, which will be required everywhere soon. Don't have any of these things because maybe you're a student who lives with your parents, or all the house bills are in your partner's name? Well, in some states, maybe you can bring along a high school transcript or send yourself a piece of mail; in others, you're going to have to call the electric company and have your name added to the account. Don't have a home at all? Again, what you can do varies by state. In some states, you can find a shelter to write a letter for you. This is great if you live in a big city or town with homeless shelters that can and will do things like that for their clients—lots of big ifs there. Otherwise . . . well, we've had to find lots of ways to prove someone's residency. We tried to get mailboxes that our clients could use, but guess what you must show to have your name added to a PO Box? Yep. ID. But let's say, for the sake of argument, that you have survived this part of the gauntlet, and now you have all your proofs of residency. Huzzah! We move on.

Most states will now ask for proof of identity, which is weird because it's almost always a birth certificate, so pretend this sentence never happened.

Now, if you have never changed your name, you are done. Congratulations. Please hold. If you *have* changed your name, I have bad news. You need the original document for every time that has happened. Every marriage certificate. Every divorce decree. Every court order. Every death certificate. If you have changed your name, you must show every time you ever changed it and why. Good times. But let's say that after months of searching and a decent amount of taco money and having to deal with one, four, or more different administrative offices, you finally have all your name change documents. Bravo. Let's go to the DMV. Folks who never changed your name, you can come too.

More than ten million Americans live more than ten miles away from a DMV, and obviously you cannot drive a car if you do not have an ID. So, let's get on the bus. Or ask for a ride. Or pay for a wildly expensive rideshare, for which you need a credit or debit card. Or hope your shelter has a van. Find a way; get to the DMV. Get there early. Maybe you're lucky and it's summer, or you live in Miami so it's lovely and warm at 7:00 a.m. when you line up outside. Maybe it's December in Wisconsin. Maybe you work from home or are unemployed or independently wealthy, so you have five hours to spend at the DMV. Maybe you don't. Maybe you have someone to watch your children or your elderly mother, who needs constant care. Maybe you don't have a disability that makes waiting in line for hours and hours impossible. Maybe. Let's say you don't have any of these issues, and you're easy-breezy and free in the summertime, and you brought a good book—a Stephen King novel, perhaps, because the only thing more frightening than the DMV is the Overlook Hotel.

And now you wait.

You scoot up in line.

You wait.

You scoot a little more.

You wait.

You realize you're hungry. It drizzles a little bit, or the sun burns, or the wind howls. But you wait. Finally, you reach the front of the line. Jack is justifiably angry at Wendy because, seriously, how rude is it to ask a writer how the writing is going while they're writing? The audacity. But you put the book down just as Danny starts his ill-fated exploration, and a woman who is, honestly, justifiably annoyed—because there is no less appreciated job than working at the DMV—takes your information, gives you a number, and tells you to go wait inside. You take a seat. Danny meets the twins. You wait. Sometime around the time that Wendy realizes that Jack has sabotaged the snowcat, your number is called. They take your documents. They take your money. Perhaps they give you an eye test. They walk away. They're gone for a while. You're not quite sure why. You start to sweat a little. Do they think your birth certificate is fraudulent? You got it from that weird website for seventy-five dollars—you sure hope it's okay. Is it that your utility bill is kind of faded because your mom is almost out of ink? Are you on the no-fly list? Are they eating lunch? Just when you're on the verge of panic, they come back. Everything is fine—twenty-five dollars, please. You pay and get sent to another line. You stand in this line for twenty minutes and then have the shortest and most demoralizing photo shoot of your life. You walk away with a sheet of paper. Your ID will be in the mail in seven to ten business days. Maybe you live in a state that knows about ID printers, and you get your ID in your hand right then and there. Congratulations. You did it.

If at this point you are still questioning why it is difficult for tens of millions of Americans to get an ID . . . stay tuned, I guess. But hopefully most of you now have a bit more understanding for how draconian this process is and why it is so impossible for so many people. In the rest of this book, we'll talk more about the people my organization has helped make it through this process, what their journeys look like, and what we can do together to make it easier for everyone in America to get the IDs they need to restart their lives.

That's the struggle that comes from not having that small piece of plastic that most of us take for granted: it puts your life on hold. That's what happened to Will. I met Will in a tent city in Los Angeles. He's a great guy—funny, talkative, will tear up at least three times in any conversation. Will has had a lot of experiences in his sixty-plus years, with all the highs and lows of life. After his divorce, his lows got very low, and then he lost his job during the COVID-19 pandemic. When I met him, he was a community leader in a tent city by the beach, just trying to find work and a home with a roof. But as often happens when you become homeless, Will had lost his ID. Without it, he was stuck. So, he kept his tent tidy, mentored some of the homeless youth, went to the beach every day, and tried to make the best of his situation. He couldn't move forward, and you can never go back, so there he was, stuck.

That's what happens when you don't have an ID. Your life

gets put on hold. You can't work, get your own housing, open a bank account, or get on an airplane. Many homeless shelters require ID for a bed, and many food banks require ID for food, so even basic survival is almost impossible. Without ID, you barely exist.

My organization, Spread The Vote + Project ID, has helped thousands and thousands of people obtain IDs. Their stories are both incredibly diverse and hauntingly similar. We work with veterans (yep—more on that later), students, seniors, people with disabilities, domestic violence survivors, people experiencing homelessness, returning citizens, victims of natural disasters, sex trafficking survivors—and the list goes on and on. All of our clients want the most basic human rights: a roof over their heads, employment, regular meals, dignity, respect, health care. But none of them can attain those things without an ID, an ID that we make incredibly difficult to get in this country.

More than 1.3 million veterans are on the Supplemental Nutrition Assistance Program (SNAP), which you probably know as food stamps. ID is required in most states to access SNAP, unemployment, and most safety net programs—the programs that are designed to help our most vulnerable people get back on their feet. Veterans have access to a Veteran ID Card, but it isn't useful for much. The Department of Veterans Affairs card isn't even accepted for all services *at the VA*. You can't use it to get a job, or housing, or SNAP. So, in a country where both political parties fall all over themselves to prove how much they care about veterans, we leave them behind. Let them starve. Watch them live in tents. If life without an ID is that difficult for veterans, how hard do you think it is for everyone else?

One of our partners is an excellent rehab program with operations across the country. People from the program called us because they had a big problem: many of the people who wanted to enter the program didn't have the ID required to cover the fees. The program was turning away people every day—people who were showing up on the doorstep seeking help—just because they didn't have ID. These were people doing exactly what we want addicts to do: recognize that they have a problem and seek treatment. But they had to be sent away. We work with the rehab program now to make sure that doesn't happen, but it is just one of many organizations that, usually because of the terms of government grants, are forced to require ID to help the people most in need. And this can often be a matter of life and death. Homeless shelters and services are also often forced to require ID for access, much more commonly than you may think. One winter night in late 2017 in West Virginia, a man went to a shelter seeking a bed. He didn't have an ID, and the shelter was forced to reject him. That night, he slept on the shelter's front stoop and froze to death.

This man lived in one of the only countries in the world that doesn't make sure that every single one of its citizens has the ID they need to live through the night. In most countries, IDs are compulsory for citizens, often for those as young as twelve or fourteen, and are distributed by local government agencies for free or a small fee. And the truth is, we have the technology required to make sure that everyone has an ID. The government knows who you are, where you are, where you were born, and what you are doing right now. The people at the DMV can pull up your birth certificate and match it with your Social Security number and one of the hundreds of photos of you that they have on file. I know this because we have had DMVs do exactly that for us more than once. There is no reason for us to make obtaining an ID as difficult as it is, except that *the difficulty is the point*. I'll explain why later, but remember that as you read the stories in this book.

The US government makes IDs impossible to get on purpose, hurting tens of millions of Americans every day.

That was the case with Isaac from Florida. Isaac's birth certificate was destroyed in Hurricane Andrew in 1992, so when he lost his ID eight years before he found Project ID, he couldn't figure out how to get a birth certificate without an ID and couldn't afford the certificate or the new ID anyway. Here's a fun experiment. Go to Vital Records and ask for a birth certificate without an ID, and then see what happens. You'll understand Isaac's problem. Isaac is on disability but could not cash his checks without his ID, and he wanted to vote but lives in a voter ID state. Without an ID, his livelihood and basic rights were impossible to access. Or take Correy, a student in Texas taking classes at Goodwill to get his GED. Correy wanted to take the GED exam, but he needed an ID to do it. Without the exam, his opportunities for getting a good job were significantly lower. His future depended on getting that ID. In Virginia, Destiny was a nineteen-year-old single mother who needed a job to take care of her son and vote for the first time. An ID for her wasn't just about her own life, but about providing security for her child and electing representatives who would make life better for both of them. All of these people are Project ID clients, people we helped get IDs so they could change their lives. For them, an ID was not just a small rectangle that sits in a wallet and gets used without really being noticed.

One of the most common responses our clients have when they get an ID is: "I'm a person again."

So, what *should* getting an ID look like? Good question. Of course, safety and security are of vital importance, and the reality is that now we have the technology to ensure both. Think about it this way. Every ten years we engage in a census because the Constitution, written in the eighteenth century, tells us to. In the eighteenth century, they didn't have a lot of things, including computers. They also had about thirteen states and, like, a thousand people, so going around counting everyone was not a big deal. It is now the twenty-first century. We have computers and a lot more people. Manually counting them is increasingly impossible. But still, because the founders told us to, we mail paper forms for people to *mail back*, and we hire people to walk around, knock on doors, and ask people questions. It's absurd, it is causing a lot of problems, and it is completely unnecessary. Mark Zuckerberg knows exactly where you are right now and what you are doing. We don't need a count. We have all of this information.

The same is true for IDs. In Virginia, we were falling all over ourselves trying to help people get birth certificates. You will read a lot of stories in this book about how wildly challenging this can be. One day we were at the DMV *again* with a customer whose attempt to get a birth certificate had been incredibly challenging. The DMV agent, who was probably just tired of seeing us, said, "Hold on, we have it in the system." *And she pulled the client's birth certificate up on the DMV computer.* Because it was there. Because all our information is there. Because if the people in charge of our government really wanted to, they could deliver a unicorn and a Ferrari to each one of us without asking us for a thing. And we know they can, because they did, when they sent us our stimulus checks. The hoops that the DMV makes us go through to get IDs is not for our safety or security.

In almost every other country in the world, you just get an ID when you hit the required age. It's just a thing that happens. You turn an age, you go to a local office, you maybe pay a few dollars or maybe you don't, and they give you an ID. If you lose it, you go back to that office. If the office staff ask you for documentation, it is minimal—because they know who you are. The government knows where you were born and what you had for breakfast and how many hours a day you play video games and your last Amazon purchase and when you last got your haircut. So they just give you an ID.

In an ideal world, when your teenage self turned sixteen, you would go to a DMV (and DMVs would be plentiful), the DMV worker would look you up on their *computer*, which is a *government computer* and has all of the *government information* on it, would verify that this person is you, would take a hideous photo, perhaps give you a driving test if you're into that sort of thing, and off you would go with your new ID. If you lost it, you would go back to that DMV, they would *look up the photo they obviously have of you*, and print you another ID. This isn't some futuristic dream in which we're living on Mars and have a female president. We can do this right now.

During my eleventy billion trips to the DMV this summer, I experienced something interesting. At that first station where I gave the worker all my documentation, I had my fingerprint scanned on a nifty little thumb-size machine. After that very first station, at the subsequent stations no one ever asked my name or to see any documentation again. They just asked me to scan my fingerprint on the same little machine I had scanned it on already. And then all my records popped up. When I got to the computer to take the written test, there was nowhere for me to type my name or any information, no printout, no confirmation number, no way for me to prove to the attendant that I had passed the test. But I had scanned my fingerprint. So, when I scanned it at the final station, she immediately knew everything about me. Quite a lot has changed about me since I was sixteen. I'm still an awkward Shakespeare-loving nerd, but now I also ride a motorcycle that scares me. You know what hasn't changed? MY FINGERPRINTS. So why do I run an organization where we must spend hours and hours and weeks and weeks tracking down documents for mostly American citizens who *have had the same fingerprints for their entire lives*? You get it. We know that we can do these things because we are already doing them. I'm not proposing major structural changes, new technology, or decreased security. I'm asking for us to use the technology we *currently have in place* while reducing the draconian requirements that make everyone's lives more difficult. It's easy, inexpensive, and would immeasurably improve the lives of millions of Americans and add billions to the economy.

This is what we can do. This is what we *will* do. We must, because Ms. Ella is not the only client we've had for whom an ID is a life-or-death need. And no one's life should depend on a tiny little plastic card. So, let's talk about IDs—who needs them, why they don't have them, how they can get them, and why this crisis even exists in the first place. This is a problem we can solve. We just need the will and the compassion to do it.

Takeaways:

1. Most Americans have government-issued photo ID and think everyone else does too.

2. More than twenty-six million American adults do not have ID, and for most it is nearly impossible to get.

3. The process to get an ID is difficult by design.

4. The US is the only country with an ID crisis.

5. We have the *way* to fix the ID crisis—we just need the *will*.

2

A Girl, a Prius, and a Half-Baked Mission

Courage allows the successful woman to fail—
and learn powerful lessons from the failure—
so that in the end, she didn't fail at all.

—Maya Angelou

Fried potatoes are, objectively, the greatest invention of mankind. We could get into a debate about which kind of fried potato is superior, the condiments with which they should be consumed, and what, if any, cheese belongs on top of them. But we all agree, with zero exceptions, that there is no greater human accomplishment than the discovery that frying a potato in hot oil, and then covering that hot deliciousness in salt, results in the world's greatest food.

So it might surprise you to learn that the first man to invent what is arguably one of the top two kinds of fried potatoes is said to have done so out of spite. Back in the 1850s, Chef George (Speck) Crum of lovely Saratoga Springs, New York, was making french fries for a Karen who kept insisting that the fries needed to be thinner and crisper. Out of sheer annoyance, Crum stopped chopping the potatoes into french-fry shape and sliced them thin, fried them to the end of their lives, covered them in salt, and triumphantly (I imagine) slammed them on Karen's table. She loved them, and Crum discovered that he had invented potato chips. This is proof, ladies and gentlemen, that sometimes Karens can change the world.

The truth is that most of our greatest discoveries come out of anger, failure, or just sheer stupidity. Mine was a product of all three.

I told you that I started Spread The Vote because of voter ID laws, and that's true. But what I didn't mention in that deeply moving introduction was how quickly we would realize that focusing on IDs for voting was like trying to end climate change because our swimming pools are getting too hot; the ID crisis was causing much bigger issues. Had I realized this in the beginning, I wouldn't have named the organization Spread The Vote at all; this is the reason our ID-related activities are now under the name Project ID, while our extensive voter turnout work is performed as Spread The Vote. I'll be referring to the ID organization as Project ID from now on, so just refer back to this paragraph if you get confused.

The first few months of the new organization were frantic. I spent every day surreptitiously taking calls in the office courtyard, on the staircase, and at the mall next door. I spoke in the living rooms and backyards of local chapters of another new organization, Indivisible, explaining our mission and asking for support. I read every book, study, Supreme Court decision, and article about voting, voting rights, and voter ID that I could find. I inhaled statistics. I found a lot of shocking ones that had, I thought at the time, nothing to do with IDs. I was wrong about that. I went to living room meetings and joined Slack channels with the leaders of other new organizations. In 2017, they were popping up like hot kernels of corn. Some were amazing. Many were unnecessary at best, potentially harmful vanity projects at worst. Several didn't make it. Others are bigger and better (or worse) than ever. I even started a podcast so that I could interview this new leadership to try to make sense of the landscape for myself and all of the people who kept emailing and texting me: *Have you heard of this group? What's happening in this state? Is anyone working on this problem?* It was a dizzying time. There was a lot of fear and confusion in the air, but mostly cold determination. If ever there was a time to gather the troops, it was now.

On the strategy side, I had a lot of work to do. By late 2016, I had identified the problem, but now I needed to build a team, find a solution, and raise money to implement that solution. The team part was easiest. The tweet really did attract a lot of attention, and soon I had an incredible group of lawyers, engineers, designers, actors, waitrons, and randos all ready to get to work. Our first task was to figure out how you help people get IDs to vote. I had done enough research at this point to know a few things:

1. More than twenty-one million eligible voters (at that point; we are now at over twenty-six million) did not have ID.

2. More than twenty states (at that point; we're now at well over thirty) had voter ID laws.

3. A few states provided free voter IDs to people who needed them.

So, we started with the most obvious task: figure out which states offered free voter IDs and how to get them. And then . . . get them? That part was TBD.

One of the things we discovered almost immediately was that those "free" IDs were kind of a joke. They were invented to get around the Twenty-Fourth Amendment—you know, the whole "no poll taxes" thing that we passed in 1962. As a child, my grandmother watched her parents count the change they'd collected in a jar in the kitchen all year so they could afford to vote. Those were the original, old-school, literal versions of poll taxes. Now we have voter ID laws, which don't say that you have to pay to vote but do say that *you have to have a thing that costs money to vote.* So, states came up with these fake IDs to skirt the Constitution. In the few states that offer these "free" IDs, they are usually almost impossible to get (worst: Georgia, best: Virginia). In the state of Georgia, you must be a registered voter and provide a document showing your date of birth, your full name, and your registered address. That is almost as many documents as are required for a DMV ID, but these "free" IDs are good for absolutely nothing except voting. You also must have transportation to a county clerk (usually) to get them, and before that you must *know* about them, which nobody does. So, we thought, if we can tell people that these things exist and help get the documents and transportation together, then our job is done! Huzzah. Celebratory drink.

Early on, I had reached out to as many voter ID experts as I could—the American Civil Liberties Union, the Brennan Center, small voting rights orgs in several states, ex-employees of grifter orgs who had seen the mess on the ground firsthand, really anyone. Our contact at the ACLU was particularly generous with his time. As my team put together ideas for how we could get people IDs, I would call him and present the plan. He would very kindly tell me that this was, in fact, a terrible idea, and here were the five hundred reasons that this exact idea had failed in the past. I would thank him for his time, weep, and then tell the team to go back to the drawing board. Not only were these early conversations critical for finally figuring out our initial plan of attack, but they also helped me understand what the larger voting rights struggle was and—crucially—why there had been such resistance to a national voter ID movement. In short, the general belief was this: establishing a national voter ID would be hard and expensive, nobody really cares about helping poor people vote, and if you tell people about barriers to voting, it will scare them, so really, it's best to pretend voter suppression is not happening. I now understand that that is only a partial explanation of the problem. It isn't *just* about our general apathy about our most vulnerable populations and our total lack of faith in the courage of everyday Americans. People really did not, and do not, have any idea about the massive ID crisis crippling our nation. And by people, I mean the general population, most politicians, most of the folks I was talking to, and first and foremost, me. At that moment, I knew less about IDs than you do.

Which is why I went to Atlanta and failed so spectacularly.

After a few months of research, we finally figured out a way to get people IDs that might work. The traditional way was to hold an "ID drive"—an event where, over one day or maybe a weekend, a bunch of people who need IDs show up, and volunteers try to help them. This is a valiant effort but ultimately doomed to fail. Our average time to get an ID, in a relatively easy case, is three to four weeks. Waiting for a birth certificate alone can take that long or much longer. If you need documents from the military or a department of corrections, you could be waiting for months. The challenges with getting an ID are so complex for so many people that for all but the easiest cases there is just no way to do it in twenty-four or forty-eight hours. ID drives were our first idea, and I have never had an idea get shot down so quickly for so many good reasons. We had to figure out how to take the full amount of time that it actually takes to get IDs for people. Finally we realized that this effort couldn't be about occasional events. This had to be something that local volunteers and staff were doing every day, every week, every month. Only if we were available to take on a client and walk them through every single step of the process—from ordering a birth certificate to picking up their ID—would we be successful. We were still thinking about the process of getting people free voter IDs, but we had no idea how crucial this line of thinking would be.

Once we figured this out, and our wonderful experts all agreed that, yes, this approach could work, we started building a plan. I would go to different cities, train people on how to get IDs (which was hilarious, because I did not know), and then those people would work in their communities and make it happen. Easy-peasy. We started a fundraiser, asking people to believe in this wild plan with zero proof of concept, and hundreds of extraordinary people helped us raise our first $14,000, enough for me to quit my job and have a few months to see whether I could make this thing real.

So I packed up my Prius. I shamefully lied to the very kind bosses at my wildly dull legal job. (I still don't know why I lied to them. I think I was afraid that if I announced that I was starting a nonprofit and then failed and had to ask for my job back, I would be embarrassed. This was not, after all, my first try, and the last time I had run an org that I believed in I got extremely ill and had to walk away.) And then I drove from Los Angeles to Atlanta, Georgia.

An important note here: Had I known then what I am writing now, I would have started right at home in LA. The need for IDs is extraordinary, and I now spend most of my days helping people on the ground in my city get IDs. But much like George Crum, I was just chopping up potatoes with no idea what they would become. So I chose Atlanta. Why? For one thing, Atlanta has an incredible voting rights ecosystem that has fought—and won—some of our toughest voting rights battles, and I knew that I could learn from the wisdom of these people. I spoke to quite a few activists and leaders in the area who told me that there was no ID operation in the city, but that they would very much like one and I was welcome. There was also a big election coming up in a few months, and I thought that would be a good test of our theory. Plus, Atlanta is also a fun city that I have always loved; it is the city where I had launched a previous start-up and had been incredibly supported and encouraged, and if I was going to go spend three months somewhere, why not in one of the nation's better towns? So off I went.

The drive across the country was blessedly uneventful. I stopped by to see my grandmother, who—not for the first time in my life— was both proud of my new career choice and also sad that I had to do this work. I come from a road-tripping family, so driving all that way seemed reasonable to me. Also, the money we had raised was not enough for me to fly to Atlanta and rent a car for three months. When the three months became six and I had been to at least as many states, I was incredibly glad I'd made this choice. The Prius is a much-maligned automobile. Does everyone in California have one? Yes. Are they a little boring to look at? Sure. Are they absolute beasts on the road that cost nothing to fill up and will deliver you safely to your destination every time? Definitely.

But I digress. I had three jobs in Atlanta: recruit and train volunteers, partner with local organizations, get IDs. The first two jobs were easy. It was with the last job that everything went terribly wrong. Our plan was this: train our volunteers about how to get voter IDs and how our brand-new software built by the amazing volunteer organization Ragtag worked, and then partner with organizations going out to canvass and register voters. As our volunteers told prospective voters about the issues or registered them to vote, we would sign up anyone who didn't have an ID and help them go through the process. Sounds perfect, right? Wrong.

A few things we did not consider that very quickly derailed us:

1. Not having an ID is a very personal thing, and it's scary and sometimes dangerous to admit it to strangers.

2. People who do not have ID are generally not on campaign target lists, which usually include only people who have voted recently.

3. People who do not have ID are not interested in getting ID to vote; they have bigger problems.

That last item would end up being the key to everything.

Our volunteers would knock on doors with canvassers and ask, "Do you have an ID?"—and then jump as doors were slammed in their faces. We had the bright idea to ask people at bus stops, terrifying them; I still feel guilty about this. It didn't help that our volunteers, wonderful as they were, were mostly middle-aged white women, chasing people at grocery stores asking them if they had an ID. I'm laughing as I type this, but when it was happening it was kind of a nightmare.

Voting organizations were also supposed to refer people who needed an ID to us. They never did. I understand now that the reason was partly that the twenty-year-olds being paid minimum wage to register voters were, understandably, not eager to add yet another thing to the list of questions they needed to ask a stranger before they ran away; even if the question did get asked, there was no way that stranger was going to give an honest response. I knew, however, that voter registration organizations were registering people who did not have ID. This was obvious from the numbers—in Wisconsin alone, three hundred thousand registered voters do not have the ID they need to vote—but I also knew because people from the organizations told me. At one organization, they even kept a list, hoping they could do something with it one day. I was gleeful when they sent me a spreadsheet with thousands of names and sat down immediately to start calling. I called. And called. And called. Few answered. The few who did hung up. No one responded to voice mail. The list of thousands led to zero leads, and I did not understand why. And then, suddenly, I did.

We assumed that people would want IDs to vote, so of course we thought that when someone said, "Hey, you know if you register, you also have to have an ID," people would sign up immediately. This assumption was very wrong.

There is a very big difference between registering someone to vote and getting someone an ID. Voter registration, if you don't live in Texas, is a quick and easy process. Fill out some info on a piece of paper or online, send it in, and voilà, you are registered to vote. It's free, it takes five to ten minutes, and in most states, it doesn't require a lot of personal documentation. You can do it with a clipboard at the grocery store. Getting an ID, even the "free" Georgia voter ID, is not like that. It requires documents to prove identity, birth, and address. And you already must be registered! This is to say nothing of the challenge of getting DMV IDs, a prospect we were only just beginning to consider.

This challenge, however, pales in comparison to the biggest issue. This was something I did not understand until I really, really did: *People register to vote so they can vote. People get IDs for life.* If you don't have the ID you need to vote, you don't have the ID you need for a job, housing, many forms of medical care, a night in a lot of shelters, food from many food banks, and so much more. Our clients need IDs because they need to change their lives, get back on their feet, feed their children. So when you walk up to someone and say, "Hey, can I help you do a lot of work to get this free voter ID?"—an ID that is good only for voting, nothing else—they are going to look at you and answer, "I need a job. I need a place to sleep. Are you going to help me with that?" After I got this response a few times, a very large lightbulb went off just inches above my head.

At the end of three months, we got zero IDs. Someone who meant well sent us a Facebook message: "How many IDs did you score?" I trembled as I tried to come up with a professional way of saying, *Zero! I failed; this isn't the kind of thing where you score.* To the great credit of the incredible friends and supporters I had in Atlanta, none of them treated me like a pariah. Every single one of them said, "This is what it's like; this is the struggle. Keep going—you'll figure it out." And I had an inkling that I was almost there.

The summer was over, I was almost but not totally out of money, and I had to decide what to do. I could have gone home, begged for my job back, and moved on. But I thought, *Fuck it, let's try Virginia.* And I got back in my car.

Takeaways:

1. It's hard to get people to think about civic engagement when they don't have food and shelter.
2. Community work has to be done in the community, by the community.

3

The Secret Is Community

Alone we can do so little. Together, we can do so much.

—Helen Keller

I was sitting in my pajamas—which we now call athleisure—scheduling volunteer trainings and meetings with potential partners when I got the call.

"Kat? Hi, it's Chris. Lori and I got three IDs."

I have no memory of what I said to Chris, but when I hung up, I ran around the apartment screaming. It was late September, and we had finally gotten our first IDs. It was all the result of the lessons in Atlanta and the self-reflection that led me to the new plan.

In the car on the way to Virginia, I thought about what we'd learned. I knew now that using voting as a way to help people get IDs was not the right approach. I knew that walking up to strangers and asking them about their personal details was almost cruel. And I knew that people desperately wanted IDs, but for things I had not considered, things I didn't even realize required IDs. I knew that I was right about the need but wrong about the method. Yet I still felt that having volunteers working in their communities was important.

The drive from Georgia to Virginia is beautiful. It's very green, the roads are pretty good, and the rest stops vary from excellent to terrifying. I'm a big fan of rest stops. It comes from spending a lifetime on American roads. One day, I'll write a coffee-table book about rest stops. I could continue to talk about rest stops, but I am the only person who is interested, so I'll get back to the point. The point is, I had a long, beautiful drive north to think about this next phase.

I am a millennial start-up kid, so I am a big fan of Eric Ries's book *The Lean Startup*, which reached bro-cult status a long time ago by creating a brilliant concept that I have more than once found to be useful: the Minimum Viable Product, or MVP. In short, the idea behind the MVP is that the old-school method of developing a business or product—spending months or years in your garage tinkering before releasing the product to the public and hoping people like it—is insufficient. You usually end up wasting a lot of time and money building something that nobody needs or wants. Say you want to build a dating app for goat farmers. You could spend a year and a half and $10 million building the app based on what you and a few focus groups think goat farmers are looking for in a soulmate, test the app with a few paid software testers, and then put it out into the world, at which point you would probably find that the app is not serving the lovesick needs of said goat farmers. *But*, if you create a bare minimum product and put it in the hands of goat farmers, you'll soon find out exactly what it is that goat farmers, and the people who love them, are looking for in a dating app. As you grow and learn and get comments and feedback, you can edit and update the app, and soon Let's Make a Kid will become the number one goat-farmer dating app in the country. It was the same story for our organization.

When we first launched, I told the team that we were at version 1.0 of what would probably end up being at least twenty-two versions before we figured out the right path. So they were all prepared when I told them that we had to change a few things about the plan:

1. We would no longer be getting people "free voter IDs." We would be getting them state-issued DMV IDs. This would take more time and cost more money than we had prepared for, but it was also the only way to get people the IDs they really needed to change their lives.

2. Trust was the biggest obstacle standing between us and the clients I knew were out there. We were never going to get anyone to confide in us by knocking on their doors or chasing them down at bus stops.

3. Our priority had to be our clients' priorities, not our political motives. Would we still talk to people about voting, register them to vote, and—as I would soon realize

was sorely needed—take the many steps needed to get them to the polls? Yes. But it would not be a requirement for our services, and it would not be our main objective. Our clients needed homes, jobs, medical care. Our only goal would be to get them what they needed. It would take us a few years to begin to change our name, but this was the moment when Spread The Vote became Project ID.

When I arrived in Virginia, I immediately began meeting with groups of potential volunteers and training them. We met in living rooms, restaurants, library conference rooms, wherever we could. The passion and enthusiasm of the volunteers stayed the same, but my approach changed. I started by talking about the need for IDs in their communities. I shared a *Washington Post* article about how difficult it is to obtain IDs and how much it matters in people's lives. I told the volunteers that 225,000 registered voters in Virginia did not have the ID they needed to vote. A Karen in the audience once told me that I didn't need to lie and exaggerate to make a point. I showed her the exact study that proved that these numbers were accurate, but as angry as I was at her approach, I wasn't surprised by her skepticism. It was very clear very early that nobody knew how big this problem was.

After I got through the basics, I told these prospective volunteers that the most important thing we needed to do was find partners. Not voting rights partners, not political groups, not voter registration organizations. Partners that were serving the same demographic we wanted to serve. Homeless shelters, food banks, free clinics. I had realized in that long car ride that we were doing this the wrong way. We needed to go where people were trusted and where we could be validated. It only took a few phone calls for me to learn that these organizations were well aware of the ID problem, that their entire communities were full of people who needed ID, and that these organizations did not have the funding, expertise, or manpower themselves to get people IDs. I found our opening.

In Arlington, we found our first partner. Fish and Loaves was a popular food bank that jumped at the chance to have us come set up a table and take on ID clients. We had just finished building our brand-new online intake form, courtesy of the hardworking volunteers at Ragtag. This incredible form, which we still use today, allows us to distill all of the information that we need to determine exactly what our clients need to get an ID into a simple online answer tree. On that first day, I had only practiced with it a few times and wasn't even sure how well it worked on mobile phones. Our goal was to arrive at the shelter a bit early, set up our laptops and paperwork, do a little on-the-ground training, and then hope that maybe a few people would show up who needed IDs.

I drove up to the church in my steadfast Prius and lugged my bags full of gear past a parking lot full of people. Inside, an incredibly kind staff member showed me to a table, and soon the three volunteers meeting me showed up. I was just about to start unpacking when the staff member yelled, "IF ANYONE NEEDS AN ID, THESE FOLKS WILL HELP

YOU." There was a rush—a *rush*—to the table, and before we knew what was happening, there was a line out the door. So much for setup and training. We grabbed our phones, pulled up the intake forms, and spent the next two hours intaking client after client after client. With no hesitation, they told us their names, dates of birth, and Social Security numbers. They pulled out long-expired IDs, Medicare cards, and tattered birth certificates. They told us their life stories—stories of loss and struggle, addiction and incarceration, and a lot of hope. Mostly hope. They asked if we would really help get their IDs and confessed that they didn't have any money. "That's okay," we said, "we'll pay for it." I did not, at that moment, know how I was going to pay for it; my poor Amex card was already straining under the weight of my now fourth month on the road. But I knew that no matter what happened, I would find a way.

At the end of the two hours, we packed up our gear, looked at one another for a long time, and told the staff member that we would be back next week. I got in my car and cried. We had finally figured it out.

These days, it feels hilarious that it was once difficult to find clients. Soon we were drowning in them. It didn't take long for people to hear about what we were doing, and soon we had partners all over the state. I was desperately trying to recruit volunteers to serve our massive list of clients. We were using social media to tell the stories of our journey and our new clients, and as a result some funds were starting to come in. Soon, someone from a family foundation called and asked if I would like a generous donation that, honestly, saved me. A lot of things were going right, but on the ID side, we had run into our next challenge.

If you go to Vital Records for a birth certificate, they ask for your ID. If you try to get an ID, they ask you for a birth certificate. The classic catch-22. To understand the depth of this problem let me give you a number: 6 to 7 percent of American adults. That's 15 to 18 million people who do not have access to birth or citizenship documents. Why don't they have them? Well, when you are unhoused, it's difficult to hold on to documents because, you know, you don't have anywhere to put them. Also, a lot of elderly people never even got birth certificates because they were born at home or were born Black in the wrong town in the wrong state at the wrong time. Currently I am working with Mr. Jefferson, a gentleman in his nineties who lives in a shelter in Los Angeles. After he was born at home in rural Texas, his parents never got him a birth certificate. He never served in the military, so we can't get him a DD214, which is often an option for older men. So with Mr. Jefferson we have to try the tortured process of getting him a delayed birth certificate, as I discussed earlier with Ms. Ella. We know a little more now, but Texas has different requirements from Georgia. As I type this, we are trying to get school records from Mr. Jefferson's primary and high schools. Wish us luck.

It's not just elderly citizens born at home. We operate in North Carolina, Louisiana, Texas, Florida, and many other states where hurricanes, storms, and natural disasters mean that people lose all of their documents every year. And then there are more dramatic cases, such as the guy who had been kidnapped as a baby and not only did not have a birth certificate, but also discovered at the Social Security Administration that his Social Security number was fake. We have a lot of clients from other countries where it can be difficult to obtain a birth certificate. Birth certificates are pieces of paper that you (might) get when you are born and that you are then supposed to keep track of for the rest of your life. I lost my remote control three times last week. Good luck with that.

Finally, one of us discovered VitalChek. For up to ninety dollars we could get birth certificates for our clients using a different method of verifying identity. It doesn't always work for everyone, but it does work for a lot of people. Luckily, we were able to pay for these birth certificates with the big grant and the growing number of donations that people were sending from all over the country. Finding VitalChek changed everything. We went from struggling to get even 25 percent of the birth certificates we needed to a success rate of about 80 percent, and our current almost 100 percent success rate is due in large part to VitalChek and our ingenious staff and volunteers figuring out the tips and tricks that help us close even the toughest cases.

Once we solved the birth certificate problem, we had to figure out how to find proof of residency for people experiencing homelessness and proof of Social Security number for people who didn't have any documents. This is a good place to talk about how this is just one of many, many ways in which we are behind almost every other country in the world.

I once tried to explain my job to a German.

"What do you do for a living?"

"I help people get IDs."

"What do you mean?"

"You know identification cards? From the government? I help people get them."

"What do you mean, you help them? You work for the government?"

"No, I run an organization that helps people get the paperwork required, pays for the IDs, things like that."

" . . . "

" . . . "

"Why?"

"Because they need IDs."

"But . . . doesn't your government do that?"

"LOL."

America is one of the few countries in the world where we believe that you have to earn the right to live. In most countries, it's just an accepted fact that people deserve health care, living wages, and the ability to get a job and housing. These are all things that all human beings need, so everyone works together to make sure those opportunities are there. Does that mean that there is no poverty, no homelessness? Of course not. But you will not find them in developed countries at the levels that we have in America and, more to the point, you will not find the barriers to escaping that poverty that you find in the US.

In no other country do families go bankrupt over health care. And in no other country are there tens of millions of adults who are unable to find gainful employment because they cannot obtain a government-issued ID card. It's just not a problem anywhere but here. I was once on a bus in Oslo. I couldn't figure out how to pay; the doors just opened and closed and people kept getting on and off without ever seeming to put money in anywhere. Sure I was missing something, I asked a hot Norwegian guy (I mean, if you have to ask *someone*) how to pay for the bus. He said, "Oh, there's a box up there." I said, "Well, I'm confused, because a lot of people don't seem to be paying." He looked at me the way Europeans look at you when you say something super American, like "How much do I pay for this very basic medical care that I just received?," and said, "Well, yeah, there's technically a fare, but we're not going to arrest people if they need transportation and can't afford it [*insert Kramer mind blown GIF*]. In other countries, just the fact that you made it out of the womb earns you the right to basic human dignity. How un-American is that?

And so we toiled, working hard to figure out every step of the process. How to get the right documents. How to pay for the documents. How to stay in touch with clients who didn't have homes, much less phones or regular access to the internet. Each step took ages to figure out, but someone would solve it, share the news, and we would all celebrate and take notes. All of which led to that incredible day when Chris and Lori called me and told me that we had finally, finally done it. We got our first IDs. From there, the floodgates opened.

Takeaways:

1. You don't know what you're doing until you get on the ground.

2. Trust begets trust.

3. Getting a birth certificate without an ID is hard.

4

Disproportionate Punishment

*The majority of people who are in prison are
there because society has failed them.*
—Angela Y. Davis, *Freedom Is a Constant Struggle*

A few blocks from my house there is what has become an all-too-familiar sight in Los Angeles and around the country: a small site with a tent, a lot of belongings, and at least one human trying to survive. This particular setup is well known in the area because it is home to sometimes dozens of bicycles, all lined up and displayed along the sidewalk. For a long time, this was just as mysterious to me as to everyone else, until I got a call saying that the man who lived there was named Ted, and he needed an ID. I met Ted at his home and, as I often have to do, set up my laptop on the sidewalk and hot-spotted with my phone to start working on his case. We chatted as I took down his details and ordered a birth certificate, and as we talked I learned his story.

Ted had a rough childhood; his brother lives in a tent a few blocks away. Ted struggles with several mental health issues, and after serving eighteen years in prison, he was released into the streets with no ID, no birth certificate, and nowhere to go. After two and a half years of freedom, he was living in a tent on the side of a busy street, repairing and selling bikes, and trying to get through each day. He wanted a home and to apply for disability, but without an ID it wasn't possible. This need had always been there, but lately it had become more urgent. Navigating home-lessness is about so much more than just finding food and a place to sleep at night. The safety issues are very real—from the bullies who claim full blocks as their territories to the weather that kills people on the street every night. A wave of crimes against the homeless had recently increased in Los Angeles, and the day before Ted and I met he had been tasered and robbed. That, along with the unusual cold and heavy rains, made it more important than ever that Ted get an ID and find a home. Of course, the process is difficult and made more difficult by Ted's situation. To get a California birth certificate without an ID, you need a notarized affidavit with witnesses testifying to your identity (I now know of an easier way for the unhoused but it still would have been almost impossible for Ted). At this point I had not yet become a notary (Ted is the reason I became one), and getting him to leave his belongings to get a document notarized was understandably challenging. Ted's mental health issues were not helped by eighteen years of incarceration or two and a half years on the streets, and it was clear that the need for professional help was getting more serious by the day. I knew I had to help Ted get an ID.

Let's take a step back. First, I'm going to assign you some home-work. I know, I'm such a Hermione, I can't help it. Go to Netflix and watch the documentary *13th* to get a small sense of what the modern-day penal system is like in America. Most Ameri-cans have no idea what goes on inside of penitentiaries. We don't know about the high costs of phone calls and emails, the regular and consistent refusal of basic rights, the slave wage prison labor that benefits massive corporations. We have largely been kept in the dark—mostly quite happily—about the realities of life in prison. We are a nation that believes that if you are in prison, you probably belong there, despite all of the statistics and stories that show the massive inequality and injustice that permeates the sys-tem. Think about this: there are people in America who are still incarcerated because of convictions during the Satanic Panic, a national fearmongering phenomenon that has been completely and thoroughly debunked by everyone from university scholars to the Federal Bureau of Investigation. If we are still jailing peo-ple who were convicted of crimes that we know absolutely did not happen, how can we possibly claim that this system is just?

The cruelty doesn't stop at the prison gates. Once an individ-ual is freed (and becomes a "returning citizen," which is how we will refer to formerly incarcerated persons in this book) the chal-lenges are just beginning. We tell RCs to get a job, find a place to live, and stay away from the people who got them in trouble—

often their family and friends. We turn them out at the prison doors, give them a parole officer to call, and wash our hands. But we don't give them an ID or any documents. So, when they go to look for a job, or a house, or any of the services they are eligible for, they don't have that little card, and they're out of luck.

Not only that, but it is almost impossible to get out of prison without owing some amount of fines or fees, and usually your ability to get a driver's license is blocked until you pay it off. We have so many clients who need fines and fees paid that we set up a separate fund to raise the often thousands of dollars that each client needs to pay to get their license, as Tina did in West Virginia. She called once because she was a returning citizen and had a fine blocking her license. She also had a baby with heart problems, who needed medication. She couldn't get the meds without a job, and she couldn't get a job if she couldn't drive. West Virginia doesn't exactly have a Metro. All Tina wanted was to keep her baby alive. Yes, this is also a comment on our health care system. Everything is a comment on our health care system. If we're not going to create a system in which we keep babies alive just because we should, the least we can do is make sure their parents have the ID they need to take care of them.

You may remember the battle for the voting rights of returning citizens in Florida, when the people of Florida elected to re-enfranchise millions of voters, only for the state government to decide that those newly enfranchised citizens could not vote until they paid off their fines and fees. The state government did so knowing that the vast majority of those returning citizens would have fines and fees that they couldn't pay—and, often, that they couldn't even figure out how to pay. We frequently have a challenge just finding out how much someone owes and in which county, and when we show up to pay the fines we know about, the clerk will pull up three more that hadn't been there before! Luckily, politicians on both sides of the aisle can agree that blocking driver's licenses for unpaid fines is harmful to just about everyone, and several states have started to ban this practice.

This neglect is how you end up with a returning citizen population that is almost ten times more likely to be homeless than the general population. This, of course, leads to the inevitable revolving door: more than 15 percent of incarcerated people were homeless in the year before they went to prison. It's difficult to stay on the straight and very narrow when you can't get food, shelter, or honest work. And with the police criminalizing everything from sleeping on park benches to public urination, it's easy to end up right back in prison before you have even had a chance to try to get your life back together. Returning citizens are set up to fail from the start, and then we blame and punish them when they do. If we want to reduce recidivism, maybe we should make it as easy as possible for them to find stability as soon as they are released—starting with providing them with an ID. Some states have started passing laws to this effect, and our political arm, Project ID Action Fund, is working to convince other states to do the right thing. This, like the ID issue as a whole, is a problem that cannot be solved by helping one person at a time get an ID. It is a policy issue that must be addressed by new and better laws focusing on what is best for the individual, the community, the state, and the country.

I know all of this now; I did not know it when I was getting started. But it took almost no time for organizations that work with returning citizens to figure out what we were doing. Soon we were partnered with a variety of organizations that help returning citizens reintegrate into society but that didn't have the funds or ability to help them get the IDs that they needed to access many of the offered services. With our partnerships, we are able to help returning citizens, often the day they are released, get started on the road to getting an ID. We soon realized that it would be even better to start earlier, before incarcerated people were out and walking around without ID. So, we started to partner with public defenders, jails, and departments of corrections, and now we are helping returning citizens in many states get started on their documents prerelease, so that we can expedite the ID process even more.

In recent years, the media and popular culture have tried to regain some balance in the way they portray incarcerated citizens, but for most of American history the belief has been that if you are in prison, you deserve to be there, and you deserve to be punished forever. This is why in most states, employers and housing authorities are allowed to ask if you have ever served time, as if having been in prison revokes your human rights to shelter and employment. Most Americans are starting to realize that the criminal injustice system has always been plagued by corruption, racism, classism, and just about every other ism, and that often those who are incarcerated probably should not have been and would not have been if they had been wealthier and whiter.

Take Dean, a gentleman in Michigan with whom we worked to pay off his fines and fees and get his ID. Dean lost most of his life to incarceration after his conviction for murder. His crime? Defending himself, his sisters, and his mother against his abusive stepfather. The jails of this country are full of women and children whose great crime was defending themselves against domestic and sexual violence. Can the state not think of a better way to manage these tragic situations? Why is prison our first resort when dealing with victims? The same goes for laws that we now know for certain were installed for racist and unjust purposes, most notably the War on Drugs. We have worked with returning citizens whose great civic infraction was possession of marijuana, an act that can still get you thirty years in jail in some states, while in others you can open an app to have marijuana delivered straight to your house. And once people get out of jail for the dangerous and offensive crime of smoking pot? They're stuck in the same trap as every other returning citizen. We don't consider the harm that these burdens do to families like Portia's; she has five children and is living in a car because she doesn't have the ID she needs to get the family into housing. Even if we don't care about Portia because she served time, shouldn't we care enough about her children to make sure their most basic needs are met?

This is a good place for me to talk about prisons, voting, and the census. Did you know that incarcerated people count as part of the population of the town that a prison is located in for the census? That means that usually very small prison towns, often predominantly white, receive more money for services, education, and infrastructure, as well as more local and congressional representation, because of the largely Black and Brown incar-cerated citizens who are involuntarily within their geographical bounds. You could win the lottery before you could find a local representative who actually visits these prisons to find out what their constituents care about, but they certainly do take the money. In every state except Maine and Vermont, currently incarcerated people who have been convicted of a felony cannot vote. However, more than 470,000 currently incarcerated people who either have been convicted of misdemeanors or have not been convicted of anything at all, and are just in jail because they are too poor to post bail, are eligible to vote. Some states, okay, mostly just Maine and Vermont, are great at making sure their incarcerated citizens vote. Most . . . not so much. So, in 2020, Spread The Vote started an initiative with Vote.org that we went on to fully manage called Vote By Mail In Jail, the only national program that works with jails across the country to help their eligible incarcerated citizens vote. This program is a lot of work—*a lot*. We have found many jails and justice systems that have been thrilled to work with us, and a few that still hold some of the worst and most bigoted beliefs about the people under their care. But even if we have to deal with a few jerks, the program is more than worth the effort. One of the best ways to ensure that a certain group has rights is to get people from that group to the polls. Let people vote in their own self-interest, rather than relying on others to do it for them. If all 470,000 incarcerated people who are able to vote actually did, the world would be a very different place.

And while we're at it, let's let people currently serving felony convictions vote too. We don't stop being citizens just because we're behind bars, regardless of the reason we're there.

Every returning citizen we meet wants to get their life back together. Believe me, nobody wants to *go back* to prison. Our client Julie in Tennessee was a recently returned citizen whose ID was not returned to her when she was released. This is incredibly common. We met her through a reentry program that helps RCs learn how to get jobs, housing, and the resources to pull their lives together. We partner with the program because, of course, many of the participants need ID. Julie needed every single document for the DMV, and we were able to help her get an ID in time for her graduation so that she could head straight out and get a job. Sometimes RCs, like our client Clint in Texas, already have a job waiting for them. Clint was a trained forklift driver who had a job offer but needed an ID to take it. He had just been released and really wanted to start working right away. We were able to help him get his ID in time for him to start his new job and his new life. The same was true for Isaac in Virginia, who had just been released a few weeks before we met him. He went to the DMV by himself with his expired ID in his hand, but they wouldn't give him a new one without all of the documentation—which, by the way, is ridiculous. Luckily, he found us through a partner, and our volunteers were very quickly able to get him the documents he needed. Sometimes the easiest cases are the most frustrating, because they are only easy for people who know the rules and the system; for everyone else the bureaucracy is impossible to wade through. Our volunteers were able to help Isaac get his ID in less than a week, which was a relief because he had a job waiting for him. And this isn't just a case of people who don't have family and friends to rely on. Most of our friends and families are not DMV experts. Take Austin in West Virginia. Austin's grandmother called us to ask if we could help get his ID after he was released. We did, and he immediately went out to look for a job. All of these people just want to work, live, and maybe even pursue a little happiness. They aren't monsters; they're probably not even mean. They are just people living in a country that, more than any other, loves to incarcerate its citizens and then keep punishing them until the day they die.

We see this shift in perspective the most with our volunteers. We have so many incredible people, who usually have never gotten an ID for a stranger in their lives before they sign up with us to volunteer in their communities. We love our volunteers so much that we've even hired a lot of them. It's always fun watching a soccer mom who had never been inside a homeless shelter—and who was a little nervous when she got trained and tentatively started working with her first client—march into the shelter a few months later, hug all of her clients and new friends, pack a bunch of burly returning citizens into her minivan, and shuttle them to the DMV. I have had so many conversations with volunteers who had no idea about the realities of the criminal justice system or had never heard the term "white privilege" until they got to know their clients, and soon these volunteers are in my inbox and on the phone with me asking me how we can make sure that no one is ever wrongfully convicted again, and is it okay if they help Jim find a job? Our volunteers are proof that once we get to know people as people, when we break down the stereotypes and the media and the hype, we realize that the guy living in the tent, the mom living in the car with her kids, the family hopping from motel to motel aren't living that way because they deserve to, or because they are lazy or evil or bad. We realize that all of us are just two disasters from being un-housed, that demographics and circumstances have much more power over our lives than we would like to admit, and that all of us—every single one of us—sometimes just needs a little help.

I'll end with Mr. Jackson, whom we met in Orlando right be-fore COVID hit. I got a call one day from Chris, our Orlando staffer, who said that he had just helped someone get an ID who hadn't had one in forty years, and would I like to speak to him? I was more than a little taken aback; this was by far the longest we had ever seen someone go without an ID. We'd had clients who hadn't had IDs for twenty or even thirty years, but forty was extreme. Forty was before I was born. Forty was . . . oh my god, was *Star Wars* even out then?? I definitely wanted to have a conversation with Mr. Jackson.

Chris got him on the phone, and right away Mr. Jackson was lovely and open and willing to tell his story. Most of our clients want us to know their stories, who they are and where they came from and why they need our help. Mr. Jackson was no different.

He told me that, not unlike most twentysomethings, he had enjoyed going out and having a good time in the late 1970s. One day, also not unlike most twentysomethings, he had a little too much to drink and then got behind the wheel of a car. On his way home, he was pulled over. A normal thing to happen, although much more likely if you're Black in any state in any decade, but especially in Florida in the 1970s. This was his first offense, but he was arrested, his license was suspended, and he was fined several thousand dollars. Mr. Jackson did not have several thousand dollars. So he never got his license back. And instead of living the long life of opportunities that he had before him the second before that cop pulled him over, Mr. Jackson was stuck—for forty years. He could never get a job that required driving beyond where public transportation could get him. In Orlando. In the 1980s. So that meant he couldn't make enough money to leave his mother's house. He never married, or traveled, or voted. He never lived his life. I asked him what he lost when he lost his license and he said, "Everything. I would have had a life." Now in his sixties, he does under-the-table cleanup work for a real estate developer. He sought us out not for an ID for a new life, but for Medicare and legal work, and so he can have a place to live after his mother passes away.

You know, it's funny. The other day I watched a movie about George W. Bush and Dick Cheney. Both had drunk-driving screwups in their twenties. Both were uninspired students in school, with limited ambition, but were saved because they were white and well-connected. Laura Bush and Ted Kennedy were both drivers in fatal car accidents in their youth. And yet they, and so many others like them, went on to have wildly privileged and powerful lives. Mr. Jackson didn't get to be president. He didn't even get to try his hand at the American dream, such as it is. He made the same youthful mistake that so many people (and, let's face it, many not-so-youthful people) do, but he lost his life for it. We got him his ID, but we couldn't give him back his time. And Ted, from the beginning of this chapter? The police performed a sweep, threw away all of his belongings, and no one has seen Ted since.

Takeaways:

1. Returning citizens are punished long after they have served their time.

2. Without an ID, it is impossible to rebuild life after incarceration.

3. Punishment in America is directly proportional to privilege.

5

Consequences of Disaster

Laws are spider webs through which the big
flies pass and the little ones get caught.

—Honoré de Balzac

A surprisingly high number of Project ID's clients are over the age of fifty—clients like Jimmy, whom we met in Atlanta when he was fifty-four. Jimmy had not had an ID in decades and didn't even know for sure what state he was born in (he thought it was Louisiana; it turned out that he had actually been born in Memphis, Tennessee). Without an ID, he wasn't able to work, so he worked odd jobs off the books, panhandled, and got caught up in drugs. Jimmy wound up in jail, and we met him through a partner program that helps returning citizens successfully reenter society. We were able to help Jimmy figure out where he was really born, get him a birth certificate and other required documents, and get him an ID. With his new ID, he got a job and housing and was able to stay sober. His ID changed his life. But the question is, Why was it so hard for him to get it when he'd had one decades before?

The senior ID gap went largely unnoticed until 2016, when the presidential election collided with the new voter ID laws, and suddenly World War II veterans and grandparents in Wisconsin found themselves unable to vote and in the news. At Project ID, we noticed that we were frequently helping seniors who'd once had that small rectangle in their wallets. They'd had driver's licenses or state IDs in the past and had found that getting a new ID, to replace one that had perhaps expired or been lost, had become difficult and often nearly impossible over the past couple of decades. The heartbreak of seniors in their eighties and nineties being turned away from the polls and then turned away from the DMV, and realizing that their vote had been stolen, was almost too much to bear. But the unifying factor was that nearly all of them *had had IDs before*. What, I wondered, had changed?

I did my research, and the answer was surprising. It used to be relatively easy to get IDs. Not a walk in the park, but not as difficult as it is now. There were far fewer barriers, fewer requirements, more state-to-state cooperation. It was possible to get an ID without a certified birth certificate, or really most of the documents that you have to show now. Getting an ID was doable for most Americans. This made sense to me because I only slightly remember getting my first driver's license at sixteen, but I do not remember needing as many documents as you do now. As a teenager who lived at home, I wouldn't have had a lease or utility bill. It's possible that my mother had my birth certificate, but given that we were an Army family, who knows whether she would have been able to find it. I had a passport and a high school transcript, but we've worked with enough high schoolers now for me to really think I would remember having to go through the journey we all took together in chapter 2. You may have the same memories. In fact, I think this is a big reason why people don't understand how hard it is to get an ID—for most of us, it wasn't that difficult the first time, and we've just been renewing ever since. Until twenty years ago, it just wasn't as hard. But then 9/11 happened. And while the country was still reeling from one of the most horrifying attacks in the history of our nation, the US government was making life a lot more difficult for our most vulnerable populations.

You may not know that the nineteen 9/11 terrorists had more than thirty IDs among them: legal, DMV IDs. They used those IDs to rent cars and board flights. They used those IDs to commit their absolutely unforgivable acts. And so the 9/11 Commission rightfully examined the process to obtain an ID as part of its review of the actions and policies that may have led to 9/11. However, we have a habit in this country of closing our eyes to danger until it happens, and then reacting in the most dramatic, over-the-top, unreasonable way that we possibly can. Unless the danger has to do with guns, in which case we just send thoughts and prayers and hope it goes away. Think about it: our social services system is not designed to make sure that everyone who needs assistance can get it; the system is designed instead to ensure that not even one person who does *not* need help gets the assistance—which would be fine, except the barriers are set so high that millions of the people who need help can't access it. Remember our stimulus checks? We wanted to be sure that not a single person who made even a dollar more than the threshold could get a payment. Never mind that during a global pandemic (1) everyone needed help and (2) anyone who got the money and didn't need it was probably going to use it to help boost our flagging economy. I spent mine on wine, but from a local wine shop because I'm a patriot. In reality, there were definitely families who made $75,001 who needed the money just as much as families who made $74,999 did. But our system is built to exclude, not include. So, when the 9/11 Commission discovered that the terrorists had used legal DMV IDs, the commissioners decided to make IDs really, really hard to get. They created the REAL ID.

REAL IDs are "enhanced" IDs that have a little gold star on them (oh, boy, was that a terrible, terrible choice) that show that the holder of the ID has provided extra documentation to prove who they are. Basically, when you go to the DMV, you'll have to show a few more pieces of documentation to double-triple prove that you really are who you say you are. As if a birth certificate, Social Security card, copy of your lease, and utility bill aren't enough, the DMV may ask for a bank statement as well. This may seem like a simple request, but think about the stories you have just read. For many people, it's difficult enough to get together the bare minimum of required documents; adding another can make the task insurmountable. REAL IDs will someday be required to board flights and enter federal buildings, which may be necessary for someone who has court dates or other reasons that they have to interact with the federal government. Many offices where you apply for social services such as SNAP and WIC (the Special Supplemental Nutrition Program for Women, Infants, and Children, a program to support expecting mothers) are in government buildings. So no REAL ID may very soon mean no government assistance for people all over the country. The REAL ID program was supposed to be in effect in all fifty states by 2005, but many states fought against the IDs, while others did not have the capacity to get their systems updated in time. The deadline has been extended and extended again. In 2020, with the deadline planned for October, COVID happened, and the deadline was pushed back two more years. As of this writing, the deadline is May 7, 2025, but we'll see what happens.

The states, however, did not wait for REAL ID to go into effect to make the process of getting an ID more challenging. Almost immediately, DMVs in all fifty states started to make big changes very quietly. They started to require more documentation: certified birth certificates or passports, Social Security cards, extra proofs of residency or identity. They stopped accepting out-of-state IDs, which used to be enough to get a new ID in most states. They started using facial recognition software to make sure your unflattering ID photo matches your other unflattering government-issued photos. They store your face in a database now, and they put lots of tiny security features into your ID that you have no idea are there. DMV IDs are the most widely used proof of identity in the country, and after 9/11 we made them highly secure and almost impossible to get.

It's important to note that when states, the federal government, and the 9/11 Commission were making or recommending these changes, they weren't doing it to purposefully prevent 11 percent of the population from being able to get IDs. They just didn't think about the people who make up that 11 percent. So now there are millions of people who did or could have gotten an ID before 9/11 who have now been iced out of the system. Project ID helps these people every day—people who have an out-of-state license or don't have a certified birth certificate, who would have been able to get an ID pre-9/11 and cannot now. Many of the elderly people whom we help get IDs had them in the past even though they had never had a birth certificate. But now, that isn't possible, and they've found themselves with a problem that they never had before. They just cannot get an ID.

My grandmother has voted in every election for fifty years. She LOVES voting. She has also had cancer several times. And she enjoys having things like water and electricity. Luckily, she is extremely well educated and well organized and probably has about twelve forms of ID, because Dorothy Tompkins never gets caught empty-handed. But whenever I read about something happening to someone elderly, I imagine it happening to my ninety-year-old grandmother, and it breaks my heart. I would do anything to make sure that she can keep voting for the rest of her life, that she always has the medical care that she needs, that she is never stuck without utilities or transportation (in many cities, seniors and people with disabilities need IDs to use the public transportation designed for them), and that she has whatever else she needs. And I'll do anything to make sure that everyone else's grandparents can too. If we all imagined these ID-less seniors as our grandparents, I bet we'd be a lot more motivated to do something. That's generally just a good rule of thumb. Imagining *ourselves* as disadvantaged and marginalized often doesn't work, because we might think, "Well, I would never be caught in that situation"—or, if you're me, "Meh, I'd probably be fine." But if we imagine our *grandparents* living on the street or unable to secure food and housing, we might react differently. Then again, if there's one thing we learned from the COVID-19 crisis, it's that a surprising number of people do not care about their grandparents—so maybe I'm wrong.

Marilyn is the perfect example of this new situation. Marilyn was sixty years old when we met her—a sweet grandmother with a silver-gray bob. Our volunteers, Tara and Deaune, met Marilyn while tabling at the downtown library in Charlottesville, Virginia. It was 2019, and she hadn't had an ID since 2004. After 9/11, Marilyn tried to get a new ID, but there was a big problem: there was no record of her birth. One of seventeen children, Marilyn had never been given a birth certificate. We knew that she *had* been born, of course; she was standing right in front of us. But we had no way to prove it. The cognitive dissonance in this business is dizzying sometimes. Marilyn had managed to get a Statement of No Record, basically the government's way of formally acknowledging that she had never received a birth certificate, but incredibly that is not enough to take to the DMV. On top of this problem, Marilyn's name was often misspelled as "Marylyn" or "Merylin" (by fans of King Arthur perhaps) or even shortened to just "Mary." Her government records were all over the place. As a Kat whose real name is Kelley—and who spells that name correctly, with *two e's*—I feel her pain. I once got a passport renewed with the abominable "Kelly" spelling, even though the government had my old passport in its bureaucratic hands when producing the new one. The DMV, however, has no sympathy, and refused to accept any of Marilyn's documents with an alternative spelling.

Before 9/11, this probably wouldn't have been a problem. When Marilyn's name showed up in the system as having previously had an ID, with maybe a couple of supporting documents, she would have been able to get a new ID. But now everyone needs a certified copy of their birth certificate. Lord help you if you are just a girl, standing in front of a DMV agent, asking them to recognize your existence. Not going to happen.

Marilyn had two important reasons that she wanted an ID: (1) her husband had passed away a few years before, and without an ID she couldn't access their joint bank accounts; and (2) her son had been in prison for thirteen years (remember, she hadn't had an ID for fifteen years when we met her), and without an ID, she couldn't visit him. So our volunteers got to work.

Luckily, a voter registration card counts as proof of residency in almost every state. Marilyn had been purged from the rolls for not voting frequently enough (which she could not do without an ID), so our team reregistered her and made sure they spelled her name correctly. Virginia also allows a piece of mail to count as proof of residency, even if it is not from a government agency, a much more generous standard than most other states. So our team sent Marilyn a letter on Project ID letterhead, and voilà, she had her two proofs of residency. Then our team had to figure out this birth certificate business. They headed to the local Vital Records office, which sent them to Richmond. That's an hour away, but they all gathered in the car, picked up Marilyn, and drove off. I have driven through almost the entire state of Virginia about one hundred times by now, and it is an incredibly beautiful, lush, green state. But that is still a lot of driving for a piece of paper.

At the Richmond Vital Records office, Marilyn and our team sat down with an incredibly kind agent who worked to help them figure out how to get a Delayed Certificate of Birth. To get this, you need three proofs of early childhood. Now, again, the sixty-year-old woman was sitting in the office. Clearly, she had lived through and survived early childhood. But that is not enough for the DMV. So, the team and the agent started to brainstorm. Luckily, her sister had had to sign an affidavit in 2005 to prove Marilyn's identity, so that was one proof. Then they found out that Marilyn had had a child at seventeen, and that child's birth certificate counted as Marilyn's second proof that *she had been alive as a minor*. So that was two; they just needed one more proof. Everyone left the Vital Records office with a little more hope in their hearts.

Next, the team checked in with a superstar volunteer, Carol, who was located in Arlington, in northern Virginia. Carol gave them some hints, and they went to the DMV with Marilyn's marriage certificate. But it was from the minister and not the state, so the DMV turned her down. But a kind DMV employee told them to try to get a certified copy at the circuit court. They went straight over, paid $2.50, and in thirty minutes they had a copy! They headed straight back to the DMV with everything they had found, and their huge pile of documents was accepted! Marilyn finally, finally got her ID.

It should not be this difficult. It should not require a group of volunteers to spend an extended amount of time Sherlock Holmesing their way through a gauntlet of challenges to produce reams of paperwork so that one kind lady can get an ID. Is security important? Absolutely. Should the 9/11 terrorists have been able to obtain as many IDs as they did? Of course not. But there is a middle ground. It is possible to make sure that every American adult has an ID while making sure that they are secure. In fact, giving everyone an ID is *the way* to make sure they are secure. If every American had a government-issued ID that was *automatically issued*, the way every other developed nation deals with ID, we wouldn't have this problem. We could ensure that everyone has the ID that they need for jobs, housing, bank accounts, and life—including the more than twenty-six million adults in America who right now do not have that ID—while also safeguarding our national security.

What would IDs for everyone accomplish, you ask, beyond helping "just" those twenty-six million people?

It's simple. We would improve employment rates, family stability, and access to health care while reducing homelessness, crime rates, recidivism, and so much more. Want a voter ID law? Fine. Then let's make sure every single American has an ID to vote with. Would it take some work? Sure. But it's possible, and the benefits far outweigh the work it would take to get there. We literally went to the moon in 1969. I know, people say that a lot, but they do so for a reason. You're deep into this book, so at this point you are aware that I'm a huge nerd. The nerds have won now, so . . . [*insert cat with sunglasses deal with it GIF*]. In all of the ways that I am nerdy, I am probably space-nerdy the most. I am OBSESSED with space. I am desperate for a chance to sign up for a one-way ticket to Mars; I would leave tomorrow. I love space and NASA, and all things space- and NASA-related, for a lot of reasons, but one of them is the extraordinary effort that it takes from so many people to get us into space and back down again. We had a lot of things in 1969: Cool cars. Sidney Poitier. The Beatles. Jell O salads. We did not have smartphones, HBO, or computers that could fit into the average American's home. The idea of going to the moon was absurd. JFK declaring in 1962 that we would go to the moon, that we *chose* to go to the moon, would be like our current president saying, "Hey folks, let's all build flying cars and give everyone a universal basic income." We still had black-and-white television! But seven years later, we did it. We walked on the moon. We chose to do it, as JFK said, not because it was easy, but because it was hard. And the knowledge, science, technology, and passion for innovation and exploration that we gained were worth every second of that hard work. There is nothing more amazing than going to space, and there are no greater humans than astronauts—except librarians. They do incredible, impossible things every day. But so do we. So *can* we.

We have achieved extraordinary policy wins in this country over and over. And here's the thing. This one thing, getting IDs into every wallet and pocket in this country, isn't even that hard. The government managed to figure out exactly how much every American made in 2019, where we lived, and what our bank account numbers were and then mailed or direct deposited checks to each and every one of us during a global pandemic. The government can absolutely throw some IDs in the mail, with a free puppy and a box of donuts.

In 2020, we had a challenge and an opportunity at Project ID. Our nonprofit organization had been helping people get IDs on the ground, one by one, for more than three years. We had thousands and thousands of stories of how challenging it was to get an ID, of how much lives change once people have one, and of how many more people needed assistance with getting IDs than the number of people we ourselves could help. I once made a spreadsheet exploring how I could get 11 percent of the population IDs. By the time I got to a staff of five hundred and a three hundred million dollar budget, I gave up, ordered a pizza, and cried. So, sure, I know I can't get twenty-six million individual human beings a photo ID—especially because more Americans turn eighteen without ID every day, so that number is growing exponentially. It's not going to happen. I'm a pretty capable girl. I'm great at finding the best new podcasts on the airwaves, I'm one of the best road trippers you'll ever meet, and I dare you to find anyone better at eating french fries than me. But getting twenty-six million plus people IDs one by one? Even Wonder Woman has her limits. Probably. No one has ever seen them.

So I knew that we couldn't, person by person, get all these people IDs, but I also knew that we had so many stories and so much proof that IDs change lives that maybe we finally had enough to create a political organization that could change policy. So, rather than getting folks IDs one by one, we could make it easier for thousands, or even hundreds of thousands of people, to get IDs with the stroke of a pen. I'd also noticed something else. There are more than twenty-six million people who do not have IDs—*voting-age people*—but when is the last time you heard a politician mention those people, or IDs, ever (unless it's in the context of voter ID, which has been very sexy lately, and which everyone is wrong about)? Never, right? Have you ever heard someone running for mayor, city council, sheriff, or governor talk about how they wanted to help the unhoused people in their districts or state get the ID they need to get jobs? Have you ever heard someone running for board of supervisors talk about starting a countywide ID program? Have you ever heard a potential attorney general talk about helping returning citizens get the IDs they need to restart their lives? Probably not. What my team and I realized is that before we can even get to the point where local and state governments are changing ID laws, we need them to know that the crisis exists in the first place. We need political parties to add it to their platforms and politicians to talk about it when they're running for office.

Because the truth is, there is no one running for office anywhere in America whose district doesn't include people who lack IDs. So the people running for office should be talking about this crisis.

With all of this in mind, our team started the 501(c)(4) nonprofit Project ID Action Fund. The difference between nonprofit organizations that fall under Section 501(c)(3) of the Internal Revenue Code and those covered by Section 501(c)(4) seems small, but it's massive. A 501(c)(3) nonprofit, like many you know and love, is allowed to accept tax-deductible donations in exchange for staying politically nonpartisan: no lobbying, no endorsing candidates, no advocating for political positions. These nonprofits are allowed a tiny gray area amount that they have to be very careful about using. The 501(c)(4) nonprofits, on the other hand, are allowed to be as political as they want, but with the caveat that donations are not tax deductible. And they have to do a little bit of charity work. There are other differences, but that's the main potato. So, with our brand-new 501(c)(4) nonprofit, the first pro-ID political organization in the country, suddenly we could advocate to change ID policy and work on the problem on a large scale.

We started with step one: endorsing pro-ID candidates, which first meant finding candidates who were pro-ID even if they didn't know it. There are a lot of great candidates who are passionate about affordable housing, increasing economic opportunities, helping returning citizens reintegrate into society, reducing homelessness, and so much more, and they just don't know or haven't been able to articulate that the crux of those problems is an

ID. When we get on the phone with them and talk them through the issues, the lightbulb goes off, and we've made a convert. We endorsed candidates in state and local elections across the country that first year, and thrillingly, most of them won! Even more thrillingly, many of them got in touch and asked how we could advise them on changing ID laws in their jurisdiction. Amazing. So endorsing candidates is a big and so far successful part of the plan. For step two, we want to change state legislation: Make it free for veterans and the unhoused to get IDs. Ban the practice of requiring IDs for basic human services. Find ways that state legislatures can make it easier for huge swaths of their populations to get the IDs they need to improve not just their own lives, but also the state's overall well-being. After all, more people with IDs means more people with jobs, which means more tax money, less petty crime, reduced homelessness (which is very expensive for the state), and so much more. It's a win-win-win-win-win. And then for step three, we are targeting DMVs, working to get them to increase the range of documents that are allowed to prove residency. We get it—they're going to ask for a birth certificate and Social Security number. But a lot of states admit so few types of documents to prove residency that we find it almost impossible for some of our clients to gather the required documents. If we can get the DMVs to change the rules, we can make it that much easier for people to get IDs.

The American identity crisis is a big problem, but realistically, there are ways to solve it. We can do so by changing policy and legislation (my real dream is for every state to automatically issue an

ID to each state resident when they turn sixteen) and by helping individuals get the IDs they need in the meantime. This is not the biggest problem that has been solved in America. It will take just as much time and effort and organizing as these changes always do, and it is certainly not something that my little team and I can do by ourselves, but it is possible. And the first step—the reason you're reading this book (thanks, by the way)—is to make sure that people know the problem even exists.

The fact that all these laws changed after 9/11 explains why nobody knows about the ID crisis: it's pretty new. We've had these drastic DMV rules for only about twenty years. It usually takes this country much, much longer to recognize a problem. Add to that the fact that the ID crisis mostly affects the poor, the elderly, the homeless, and all manner of other groups of people who are generally invisible, and it suddenly becomes very clear why no one knows about the ID crisis in America and why the government hasn't done much to address the issue. I wouldn't even know about it if I hadn't decided to get into the voter ID business. More than twenty-six million adults in this country do not have photo ID, and yet the vast majority of the rest of the population hasn't a clue that the problem exists. But it affects us all, whether we know about it or not.

If the global pandemic reminded us of anything, it's that we are all living in a community, and we are affected by the actions of others—and not just in terms of public health. We are all in this economy together, and we are dragged down or lifted up by the number of people who are actively engaged in it [*insert cliché about high tides and all boats*]. We are all impacted by how many people are paying taxes and spending money at restaurants and going to the doctor and living in safe and affordable housing. These things affect how well maintained our roads are, how good our public schools are, how quickly a pandemic spreads, how safe our neighborhoods are. The more people who have steady jobs and fair pay, the better it is for all of us. So, when more than twenty-six million adults cannot work or sleep under a solid roof or seek medical care or open a bank account, it affects all of our lives, whether we like it or not. We can bury our heads in the sand and pretend we don't see the problem, but while our heads are in the sand, that problem is coming for our bank accounts, our home values, and our public health systems. And that means that even when we are reacting to horrifying events, we have to react in a way that *helps* the most vulnerable members of our society, not in a way that harms them.

Everything changed overnight on 9/11. It happened my first week of college, and like most Americans, I thought I had seen and understood the consequences. But the thing I am learning every day is how many of the changes I didn't see. Sure, I knew that airports, my second home, were suddenly far less friendly and didn't really feel any safer, but I didn't know until law school how much 9/11 impacted my personal privacy. I knew that politics suddenly felt more vengeful with less reason, but I didn't understand how treacherous the Patriot Act really was until I studied it. I thought I knew the impacts of 9/11, and now I know that I never fully will.

The older I get, the more I realize that the consequences are in the details. We make hasty decisions and then realize years later that we had no idea what the results would really be. Just look at how the decisions we made about how we would feed our nation fifty years ago impacted our long-term health, or how building a nation of cars impacted global warming. We have no idea what impact our decisions are going to make, and it is always the people with the lowest incomes, who are in the most vulnerable positions in this country, who feel the effects first. First, but not exclusively: the effects don't stop there. Eventually, these things affect all of us. So, yes, it was much easier for you to get a driver's license when you turned sixteen than it is now. And that fact is keeping tens of millions of Americans from participating in the society that is supposed to be protecting them. And *that* is impacting every single one of us, every day.

Takeaways:

1. The ID crisis was created after 9/11, when IDs were made much more difficult to obtain.

2. Senior citizens have been significantly impacted by the ID crisis.

3. It is possible to make IDs safe while also ensuring that every American has one.

4. The ID crisis affects all of us, whether we have an ID or not.

6

Serving Those Who Served

You will never do anything in this world without courage.
It is the greatest quality of the mind next to honor.

—Aristotle

Mike was a young veteran, a Marine who served in Afghanistan before ending up in Miami. Like many vets, he struggles with post-traumatic stress disorder, and he was living on the beach when we met him. Mike was from Florida but hadn't had a Florida ID in many years. He wanted to rent a room, apply for disability, and get his Patriot Pass yearly bus card, but you need an ID to do any of those things. When Kristina, our Miami staffer, met him, he was struggling and needed to get shelter and assistance as quickly as possible. There were some ups and downs, and it took two full months (a month and a half of which was spent waiting for his birth certificate), but Kristina was able to get him all of his documents and get an ID in his hands. It cost us $46.89, an amount that would have been impossible for Mike to handle alone. A veteran, a Marine, a man who served our country in a war halfway across the world came home and had no one to help him acquire the basic human rights that he fought for. The way we treat veterans in this country is criminal, it is hypocritical, and it is worse than you think.

I grew up on Army posts, and almost everyone in my family is a veteran or has worked or does work on a military installation. My grandmother went to North Carolina Central University (go Eagles!) for undergrad and grad school, became a librarian—or in other words, joined the ranks of the greatest people in the world, along with nurses and astronauts—and got a job as a civil service librarian. My grandmother is over ninety and can still tell the entire story about applying for the job, even though her skeptical roommate said, "Dorothy, it doesn't say this job is for Coloreds"; my grandma, being my grandma, said, "I'm applying anyway!" She interviewed, got the job, and was told that she was moving to Okinawa, Japan, immediately. My great-grandfather had to call a friend to get back a suitcase he had lent the friend years earlier, and within weeks, my grandmother was on a plane. She landed in Hawaii and got to spend a few hours marveling at how beautiful it was before she got on a second plane and landed in Okinawa. I visited Okinawa a few years ago to see it for myself, and it truly is one of the most beautiful and romantic places in the world. I very quickly understood the next part of my grandmother's story, the part where she met a tall, gorgeous soldier who looked like A-Rod, immediately married him, and then immediately had four daughters. It's exactly the kind of island where that sequence of events seems not only possible, but probable. My family eventually ended up in Sierra Vista, Arizona, because it is right next to Fort Huachuca, home of the Buffalo Soldiers (Google it), but also the last place my grandfather was stationed. To this day, our family's small town in Arizona is connected to that Army post, where my aunt now teaches. And me? Well, I spent the first half of my childhood on Army posts listening to "Taps" every day at 5 p.m., leading General Rainbow Brite and her My Little Pony army into battle against the evil G.I. Joes (they kept flushing Ken's head down the toilet, but my team of Barbie medics fixed him up as best they could) and getting my very first military ID card at ten years old. So as someone whose entire life and history is wrapped up with the military, it both broke my heart and enraged me when I found out how badly we treat veterans in this country.

"But wait," I can hear you say, "Veterans *do* get IDs! They get veteran's IDs at the VA. You probably don't know about that, even though this is your job, which is why I am sending you this email." That is a direct quote from at least one email in my inbox every day. But I digress. Let's talk about VA IDs.

Yes, the US Department of Veterans Affairs does have IDs just for vets. They're great! They get you 10 percent off at Red Robin and most sporting goods stores. There are three different types of VA IDs, and *all three of them require a veteran to have government-issued photo ID to get the VA ID.* What are these IDs?

1. The Veterans Health Identification Card (VHIC), which is the veteran's key to checking in to appointments at the VA, getting on base, using the commissary, shopping at the post or base exchange, and other services, and which you can get only if you have a service-connected disability rating under 100 percent, which is difficult to get the VA to approve.*

2. The Department of Defense ID (DODID) card, which can be used to get access to services on military installations and is available only to those with a 100 percent disability rating.

3. The Veterans ID Card (VIC), the most popular of the three, which provides access to discounts at private businesses.

Here is a list of the things you cannot do with all or at least one of these IDs:

- Prove eligibility for state or federal benefits
- Present as a form of identification at the airport
- Use the VIC to check into the VA hospital

---

* The ratings system is confusing and is tied to disability compensation, but what's important here is that you have to have a disability that has been approved by the government to get one of the first two IDs listed here. And the government really, really does not like approving veteran disabilities.

- Show as proof of retirement from the Armed Forces
- Get access to military installations with the most popular card, the VIC
- Get a veteran's designation on your DMV ID

So, to sum up, the Veterans ID Card cannot help veterans get jobs, housing, or government benefits. The VIC was created only in 2015, with the specific purpose of making it easier for veterans to get discounts from private businesses. It was another attempt by politicians to look as though they were really helping vets out without actually doing anything to help them.

What does this mean for veterans who are struggling? Well, more than 1.2 million veterans are on the Supplemental Nutrition Assistance Program, or SNAP. This means that they are living below the federal poverty level, which, as we all know, is a criminally low estimation of how much it really costs to live in this country. This means that veterans like Liz, in Virginia, may have a home but struggle without access to a fully functional government-issued ID. When we met Liz, she hadn't had an ID in nine years and was just managing with her VA ID. Liz has chronic arthritis and needed a walker for mobility. Her VA ID enabled her to access her medications, but what she really needed was to qualify for an assisted living home. Her VA ID would not help her with that. Even though Liz was a veteran with a valid VA ID, we still had to go through the entire process of getting her documents to get her DMV ID. Luckily, Liz had a lot of documents already—a benefit of having a home is that you have a place to store things—so our volunteers helped her put together all of her documents and took her to the DMV. As a result of some challenging handwriting caused by Liz's arthritis, along with some questions about her birth certificate, our volunteers had to beg, plead, and get the supervisor involved in order to get the DMV to approve Liz's documents and give her an ID. This was a veteran with a valid VA ID in her hand. After nine years of struggling, Liz finally got the fully functional government-issued ID that she needed. How on Earth can we say we care about vets when we make them go through all of this?

And then of course we have the dual shame of veterans without IDs who are also unhoused. More than 40,000 veterans are experiencing homelessness in the US (this, like all of our homelessness counts in this country, is a number that should be looked at with extreme skepticism). Veterans are *more likely* to be homeless than nonvets: 21 out of every 10,000 veterans are homeless, compared with 17 out of every 10,000 nonvets. And that's just the average. The numbers are much worse for veterans of color. Thirty-three out of every 10,000 Hispanic or Latino veterans, 56 out of every 10,000 Black veterans, 88 out of every 10,000 Indigenous veterans, and 105 out of every 10,000 Native Hawaiian and Pacific Islander veterans are homeless. Those numbers are staggering and shameful, and I should note, these counts were made *before* we got hit with a global pandemic that significantly increased joblessness, evictions, and thus homelessness across the country. These unbelievable rates of homelessness among vets also explain why so many of our clients are veterans who fit into many other categories. Most of our veteran clients are also unhoused, returning citizens, recovering, or all of the above. If we can't even pass policies to help our vets, what hope does anybody else have?

Remarkably, veterans even need IDs to access services specifically *for* veterans. Dennis was sixty-two when we met him and had become homeless after a divorce. He wanted to get into transitional housing for veterans but couldn't without a government-issued ID. And no, a VA ID wouldn't cut it. Dennis couldn't get food stamps or a room in a hotel or even donate blood for extra income without an ID. And even though he served this country, he couldn't get anyone to help him get any of those things *without an ID*. Of course, then there's Kyle, who had a job offer *at the VA* but couldn't take it until we helped him get an ID. It's important to remember that IDs aren't just for jobs and housing. You need ID for most major life milestones. Our client Terry is a Vietnam vet and Purple Heart recipient who was blinded in combat. He met Leslie at a conference for blind vets in the 1970s; decades later, they rekindled their romance, and Terry moved across the country to marry her. One problem: you need an ID to get a marriage license. Terry and Leslie tried to get his ID on their own but faced obstacles along the way. They finally found us and we were able to help them get the ID that would allow them to restart their lives together. Veterans deserve jobs, food, housing, all of that. But they also deserve love and happiness and the right to get married.

Every other Thursday I volunteer at a large housing and services complex for unhoused veterans in Los Angeles. I set up at a table in a midsize conference room and help the residents of this bright and sunny building, snuggled between warehouses and directly under the LAX flight path, get their IDs. In California, a veteran can use their DD214 (military discharge papers) as proof of identity to get their ID. It's great if a vet happens to have that and not their birth certificate, but if they don't have a DD214, getting it can take forever. You would think that any of the veteran's services employees who work with these gentlemen (at this facility, they are all male; women and children have a different housing complex in another part of town) could just pull up their paperwork online and print it out, but that would be too easy. This is the military, after all. On Tuesdays, I drive the veterans who have all of their documents to the DMV. They usually don't talk about their service much, but they do talk about what they want to do next: start a business, get a job, see their kids. At the DMV once, an employee refused to accept a DD214, even when I showed her exactly where on the DMV website it lists the DD214 as an acceptable document. She made up a lot of fake reasons that she couldn't take it and finally accepted the document only because, as the veteran said, "I think you scared her." I sure hope I did. When we went to the next window and had to go through the whole thing again, I added "losing my temper at DMV employees" to the list of things to talk to my therapist about. Mostly though, the process goes smoothly. It costs five dollars and requires a signed paper from a veteran's service official to get the "veteran" designation on an ID in California. All of the vets want it, so the staff and I have worked out a good system to make sure they get it.

The vets are without a doubt my most polite clients. A lot of the older men are hilarious; one is using the last of his G.I. Bill benefits to go to music school, and while we were at the DMV, he stood around in his porkpie hat making up songs and doing outrageous accents. The DMV employee didn't think it was funny, but we had a great time. A lot of the younger guys talk about injuries they sustained while deployed and how they are working to get the medical care they need so they can get back on their feet. The staff at the shelter are incredible; they really deeply care about the veterans and work hard to help them get the resources they need. When I had a client who was in his nineties, had cancer, and was living in a tent on the street, they leaped up to do what they could for him. He wasn't getting treatment for his cancer because he didn't have any documents to get an ID to be treated at the VA, so we worked together with his case manager to get him housed, get his DD214 and birth certificate, and get him help. The staff, who found me out of the blue, work hard to find as many outside resources as they can. Most weeks I share the conference room with an accountant who helps the vets with their taxes, and they frequently hold job fairs. The challenges don't always seem big at first blush. One client had a small problem. He had an ID, but the DMV had neglected to add the second part of his last name. Near tears, this veteran in his seventies looked at me and said, "I served this country, I won a medal—why won't they get my name right?" I assured him that it wasn't personal and was just one of the hazards of bureaucracy, but when you went to war for a country and the government can't even get your name right, it actually is personal. All of it is deeply, painfully personal.

Our country has two political parties that fall all over themselves to be the most veteran-loving patriots, all the while standing by and letting those same veterans fall by the wayside. Our political arm, Project ID Action Fund, is working hard to convince state legislatures to pass legislation that would make DMV IDs free for every single veteran in the state, regardless of income or disability. Veterans shouldn't have to prove that they are poor, or unhoused, or disabled to get the ID that will allow them to pursue the rights they fought for all of us to have. Even when Congress *does* address the issue of veteran homelessness, it completely misses the mark. The Reaching Every Homeless Veteran Act of 2021 is a fantastic attempt to address the homeless veteran crisis—*except that it doesn't address their lack of IDs*, which of course they need to access any of the solutions covered in the bill. National ignorance of the ID issue is leading us to make fatal mistakes and pass federal and state legislation that completely fails to help the people it targets. At some point we have to look at the most fundamental part of the problem—the lack of IDs—and choose to address it. What does it mean to be a country that doesn't take care of its veterans? And how can we expect that country to take care of anyone else? At Project ID, we've seen how veterans can change their lives with an ID. What would happen if this country decided that every single person who served should just get one, automatically, for free? Haven't they earned that?

Takeaways:

1. America treats veterans abominably, and they are suffering because of it.

2. The VA card is not the same as a government-issued photo ID.

3. If we won't even help veterans, what hope does anyone else have?

7

The Kids Are . . . Fine

Kid, you'll move mountains.

—Dr. Seuss, *Oh, The Places You'll Go*

Getting a driver's license is a classic rite of passage in America. We are a car nation, after all. When you turn sixteen, you get a license, the end. If you're lucky, you get a car. Most of us just drive our mom's car to pick up milk for her and chauffeur our younger brother around. Maybe that was just me. So, you may be surprised that for young people these days, turning sixteen doesn't necessarily have anything to do with driving. Gasp! *I know.* Can you imagine?

It's been largely underreported that sixteen-year-olds aren't getting driver's licenses as much as they used to. In 1983, 80 percent of eighteen-year-olds had driver's licenses. In 2018?

Sixty-one percent. Forty-six percent of sixteen-year-olds had licenses in 1983, compared with just 25.6 percent in 2018. Older adults' possession of licenses has not followed the same trend, decreasing by just 4 percent. Why are teenagers not getting licenses? Many public schools are no longer teaching driver's ed, and the cost of private driving schools, cars, insurance, gas, and so on has priced many teenagers out of that age-old rite of passage. Add to all that the prevalence of rideshares and real concerns about climate change, and it's no surprise that teen driving rates are plummeting. The problem is, when teens don't get driver's licenses, they often don't know that they still need to go to the DMV for a state ID. When Project ID goes to high schools, we find that most seniors do not have ID. This becomes a real problem when they want to get jobs and start their lives. It's such a huge challenge that we have partnered with full school districts to help all of their high school students who need IDs to get them. Schools just do not have the money, time, resources, or expertise to do it on their own, and many young people do not have parents who are in a position to figure out how to get their birth certificates, navigate the rules of the DMV, and provide the funds. Many people don't even know that a non–driver's license ID is an option.

Kendra was in this situation. She was a student in Detroit whom we met through our partnership with the Detroit Public Schools. Kendra's student ID didn't have a photo, and she wasn't able to use it off campus for most things, including getting a job. She had no idea that there was another option until she found out about our program through her school literacy club.

When we helped her get her state ID, for the first time she had what she needed to work. Then there's Melissa, who needed to take the SAT but didn't have a photo ID to do so. She didn't know this was a problem until she had already scheduled her first exam, so she had to miss it; luckily, then she found us. Her parents were organized and had her documents ready, so it took us almost no time to get her an ID, and she was able to take the next available exam. Melissa wanted to go to college, but without an ID, that almost wasn't possible.

For a lot of young people, getting an ID is the biggest key to the stability that they do not have at home. In our earliest days, we part-nered with a youth shelter, which is where we met Christie. Christie was living at the shelter and needed an ID. Her bag was stolen with all of her documents in it, and she desperately needed to make safer living arrangements and get a job. Going to her parents for help was not an option, but luckily, we had just started working with her shelter. We helped Christie get an ID, and our volunteer even found her a family to live with and then, when the next election arrived, took her to vote for the first time. Christie had her whole life ahead of her, but without an ID she was stuck.

We as a nation are doing a huge disservice to vulnerable youth, especially if they are unhoused or foster kids. Project ID works all too often with young people in the foster system, who are forced to exit the system as soon as they age out but who have no documents with which to start their lives. We rarely give foster kids IDs when they age out, and if they haven't found a family, they may not have anyone who can help or support them. Within four years of aging out, 50 percent of former foster kids have zero income. The ones who do average an annual income of $7,500. When I worked with Wallis in Long Beach, she needed her ID before she graduated from high school. Referred to us by the local children and family services agency, Wallis was living in an unstable situation, was about to graduate from high school, and really wanted to be able to get a job to support herself. We were able to get her birth certificate and ID just before she graduated, giving her that much more of a chance at a happy and stable life.

We also, appallingly, work with a shocking number of people who were adopted as children only to have their adopted parents kick them out the day they turned eighteen, which is what happened to Lewis in Fort Worth. Lewis's adopted parents dropped him off at a homeless shelter on his eighteenth birthday. He was still finishing his senior year of high school. It was so difficult to get him a birth certificate that we had to work with his state senator to make it happen. After our intrepid Fort Worth staffer and favorite team grandmother, Kat, got Lewis his ID, she was able to work with an organization to escalate his housing request to get him into a home as quickly as possible. Lewis was a good student with a goal to become a personal trainer for athletic teams, and it was almost derailed by the callousness of his adopted family. This heartbreaking cruelty leaves some of our most vulnerable young people without anywhere to go and, usually, without the ID they need to find a job, a home, and any way to build a life for themselves.

The rules at some state DMVs are almost designed to exclude young people, especially when it comes to the kind of documents these agencies will accept. Luke, a student in a transitional program for young adults with disabilities in Nashville, was born in Mexico and didn't speak much English, but he had more documentation than almost any other client in our history, including a Mexican passport, birth certificate, US work permit, school ID, and more. However, he didn't have proof of residence, because he lived with his parents. Every time we went to the DMV they told us something different: first they said we could use his parents' pay stubs and utility bills if we had his birth certificate translated to English; then they said we could use his parents' utility bills only if one parent came with him to the DMV, which was impossible because they worked full-time and didn't speak English—besides, Luke was eighteen and didn't need a parent to sign for him. Even though Luke was a student in the Metro Nashville Public Schools, the DMV would not allow him to use documents that we knew we had been able to use with students who were born in the US. We were turned away every time we went. Luckily, in the midst of this chaos, Luke got a job with his work permit. Once he had his own pay stub, our staffer spent hours at the DMV explaining the situation over and over again. We finally got his ID, but the process should not be this difficult.

Speaking of vulnerable youth, we don't talk about children in juvenile detention, but we need to. April made some mistakes in high school and ended up in juvenile detention. When she was released, she moved in with her grandmother and tried to get her life restarted. She wanted to go back to school and sign up for social services, including medical care, but of course, she didn't have an ID. We don't give returning citizens IDs when they are released in most states, but to not help juveniles get back on the right path after release is particularly cruel. More than forty-eight thousand American youth are in confinement every day in the US. Twenty-six percent of those are incarcerated pretrial, by the way, so we're locking up kids before we even convict them of anything. The majority of these young people come from unstable homes (and again, not because kids from unstable homes are more criminally inclined than kids from stable or wealthier homes, but because those more privileged kids almost never end up in detention for the crimes they commit). Sixty-five to 70 percent of those children have diagnosable mental health conditions, and frequently we're just arresting them because there are no mental health services available. When these extremely vulnerable young people are finally released back into the world, they are given varying degrees of services and support depending on the state and city that they live in, but nowhere near enough anywhere, and—you already know what I'm going to say next—they do not have the documents they need to start over. Project ID partners with a juvenile reentry program in New York that helps these young people with the services and support that they need for a real chance at a strong new beginning. They called us because IDs are such a big problem. They shouldn't be.

So much of this issue is about socioeconomic status. Poor students often do not have parents who can afford IDs and documents; the parents may be incarcerated, may not speak English, or simply may not be able to take the time off work to take their children to the DMV. Twenty thousand young people a year age out of foster care, and they do not leave with the IDs they need to enter adulthood. This issue is doubly compounded for children with disabilities. When I worked with Henry, a student at the local public school for children who are deaf, he was nineteen and graduating from high school in a few months. His father didn't have a car or the money to get his birth certificate or ID, and it took Henry, a school counselor, Henry's interpreter, his father, and me working together to get Henry his ID. The barriers for Henry were already high, but his family's financial struggles, which are normal for a huge percentage of Americans, made those barriers even higher. I had recently helped another deaf client get an ID, a woman in her forties named Rachel. Rachel lived in a tent in Skid Row in the "red light" area. It could not have been a less safe place for a deaf Black woman to live. Her boyfriend had stolen everything she had, she didn't have any family to call on, and she struggled to make herself understood in writing. It took ages to get her birth certificate, and when we finally went to the DMV, Rachel's case manager and I celebrated. The road out of Skid Row and into stability will be that much more difficult for Rachel, and as I worked with Henry, I remembered how much we fail children with disabilities in this country and how much socioeconomic status plays into all of these issues. The fact is, IDs are not a problem for wealthy or even many middle-class children. IDs are a problem for our most vulnerable children, the ones we should be helping the most but usually end up just leaving behind.

I'll leave you with Kevin. When we met Kevin, he was in his early thirties, and he sought our help to get an ID. Kevin had no documents, was homeless, and lived forty minutes away from the nearest DMV. Having grown up between foster care and a great-grandmother, Kevin didn't know much about his own past. He didn't even know why he had been given up by his mother until we got him a birth certificate, his first, and he found out that she had been twelve and his father twenty-two when he was born. When Kevin got his ID, he said, as so many of our clients do, "All right! I exist again!" He and his fiancé, for whom we also got an ID, were able to take the jobs they had recently been offered, find a home, and start their lives together. My hope is that we can get IDs for kids like Kevin long before they are thirty and unhoused.

That's the goal here. That's why I am writing this book. Because we need to get IDs for those who do not have them, but we also absolutely must close this gap and make sure that no one ever goes without an ID again.

Takeaways:

1. Young people are not getting IDs at the same rates that they used to.

2. Foster children are released from the system with no documents and feel the impacts for the rest of their lives.

3. Poor students suffer from a lack of IDs at much higher rates than wealthy or even middle-class students, setting up yet another achievement gap.

8

The Invisible Disabled

Accessibility allows us to tap into everyone's potential.

—Debra Ruh

Jennifer Costa has worked for Project ID since almost the beginning. She was our volunteer director for many years before jumping over to development. Over the years we have become good friends, even as I fear for her life every time she sends me a picture of an alligator crossing the street. Or crocodile. Whatever they have in Florida. I refuse to Google it. Jennifer used to run a homeless shelter, has published two books, and is generally one of the most humbly accomplished people I have ever met. She also has three children with disabilities and could easily rewrite every law covering health and disability in Florida, because she knows them all, and all of them are terrible.

So I was surprised when Jennifer was suddenly having an ID challenge. Of all of the people in Florida, Jennifer is the least likely to need help getting an ID. But here's the problem. The ID wasn't for her. It was for her nine-year-old daughter, Laura, a hilarious little girl who loves to entertain us during Zoom meetings. She has nonverbal autism and sometimes has challenges walking long distances from cars to buildings. So Jennifer tried to get a disability placard for the car. But the person with the disability needs an ID, or a doctor to verify their identity . . . with an ID. But Laura is nine. There aren't a lot of nine-year-olds running around with an ID. So Jennifer took Laura to the DMV—where the DMV insisted on "verifying the authenticity" of the letter from the doctor.

Once the letter was "verified," the DMV worker asked Laura a series of questions. Laura is nonverbal. The DMV worker presumably knew this, because the doctor had just verified it. But still, they tortured and humiliated the young girl by asking her questions that she could not answer. Then, because they hadn't hurt her enough, they asked for her signature. She was nine. In the end, after her paperwork was accepted, Jennifer had to call a supervisor before they would finally allow her to stand just outside of the frame of the camera while the terrified and now traumatized little girl got her photo taken. To you, this might be horrifying. To a person with a disability, this is just another Wednesday.

Given how little research there is on IDs in America, you will not be surprised to learn that there is almost none on how many people with disabilities do or do not have IDs. A lot of our answers must be gleaned from research about voting. In 2012, the Pew Research Center found that 7.2 percent of registered voters with disabilities did not have photo ID, compared with about 4.5 percent of nondisabled voters. At Project ID, we do not ask people about their disability status, and yet at least 15 percent of our clients have informed us that they have a disability; dozens of our partners work specifically with people with disabilities. If you work with people with disabilities or have a disability, or maybe if you have a family member with a disability, you are well aware of how difficult it is for them to get IDs. If you don't, then you don't, because I would argue that there is no group of people more invisible in this country than the disability community.

America is hostile to most groups—Indigenous Americans, obviously; women; women with children; women without children; people who rent their homes; people who can't afford large spikes in their adjustable-rate mortgages; people who like health care; people who like food that doesn't poison them; and, remarkably at the very moment in history that I am writing this, babies who enjoy eating. But I think it is safe to argue that there is almost no one America is more hostile to than people with disabilities.

To begin, let's look at the process to apply for Supplemental Security Income (SSI), which you've heard of as disability benefits. SSI is our benefits system for children and adults living with disabilities who have limited incomes. Applying for it is a living hell, *and* 72 percent of applications are denied. I can assure you that well over half of the people applying for SSI are not putting themselves through that nightmarish experience for fun or for the paltry, paltry sum they will receive on the off chance they are accepted. Social Security Disability Insurance (SSDI) is for people who have worked (you get actual work "credits") and paid into Social Security. The rejection rate for SSDI is a little better, at 55 percent. The average wait time for an SSDI appeal in 2019 was 506 days, so good luck eating for a year and a half. Maybe that's why 110,000 people died while waiting for a decision on their appeal between 2008 and 2019 and 50,000 applied for bankruptcy between 2014 and 2019. And that was before the pandemic, when the Social Security Administration shut down its offices for a full two years.

So, what are some ways that you can be accepted? Well, first of all, it's really important that you don't have any money. If you or your parents or your neighbors or your dog's babysitter have any savings or maybe a college fund or maybe just a decent-paying job, you're going to want to throw all of that money into the river. If you're not impoverished, the government can't force you to stay impoverished, and people with disabilities are not allowed to have nice things. So go ahead and "spend down," which is what they call it when they want you to take all of your savings and spend it on Nintendo Switch games. I recommend *The Legend of Zelda: Breath of the Wild.* It's really hard and you can play it for the rest of your life and never win, which is great because this is the last fun thing you will ever be able to afford. You are 100 percent not imagining the right number, so I am just going to directly quote the Social Security Administration here, in possibly the most John Oliver moment of my life:

> *To qualify for SSI, you must also have little or no income and few resources. The value of the things you own must be less than $2,000 if you're single or less than $3,000 for married couples living together. We don't count the value of your home if you live in it, and, usually, we don't count the value of your car. We may not count the value of certain other resources either, such as a burial plot.*

They may not count the value of your burial plot.

Those amounts have not been changed in forty years. You're starting to see what I'm talking about, right? If not, you're like the people on tour with me at Monticello, who looked around the slave cabins and said, "Not bad, it's pretty roomy." True story.

Okay, so you've "spent down," and now everything you own, including possibly your burial plot, is worth less than a 1974 Pinto wagon, and your most valuable possession is now the one avocado you can afford a month. What next? Well, obviously you have to prove that you're disabled *enough*. Bonus points if your death is imminent. Yes, you have to be evaluated and judged. No, it will not be fast: three to four months at the least. But don't hold your breath, because you will almost certainly be denied. Maybe you can use some of that avocado money for a lawyer. It will increase your chances, but you know, you're poor now.

But look at you, fancy pants. You did it! You beat the system and got that oh-so-rare acceptance letter. How many buckaroos are we looking at? It must be a lot, if the government is making such a big deal about it. Where do you sign for your brand-new Rolls Royce and smells-like-new McMansion? Just kidding— obviously. The maximum SSI benefit in 2022 was $841 a month for singles and $1,261 a month for couples. That's without state supplements, which range from zero dollars and zero cents to some dollars and cents but with a variety of restrictions, to a more humane supplement in states such as Hawaii and New Jersey that apparently don't want all of their disabled residents to starve to death. Oh, by the way, that federal payment? It's below the federal poverty line. Well below.

Maybe you're thinking that this can work out if the recipient can get a small side job. The government thought of that too. If you want to keep your poverty benefits, don't even think about working. Don't sell that crocheted potholder on Etsy. Don't get paid to speak about nuclear fission. And don't get married. Quickest possible ways to lose your SSI and even your life-saving health insurance.

"So what does this have to do with IDs?" you may be asking, with your cold, cold heart. Well, hopefully it's pretty clear. People with disabilities already face a huge range of challenges, both because of their disabilities but also mostly because of ableism and the fact that people can be real jerks. I have been to the DMV with members of the deaf community, people with a wide range of mobility issues, people with varying levels of mental illness, and it is rare to find a DMV that is truly set up to accommodate people with disabilities according to the requirements of the American Disabilities Act, and far less common to find employees who are trained to act like actual human beings. But, on top of all that, when we are forcing people with disabilities to live in abject poverty, then we see all of the issues that we have discussed in this rest of this book that lead to people not having the ability to access an ID. It's no wonder that several of the clients I have spoken about in other chapters are living with disabilities. Go back and see how many times I mentioned the word "disability" before this chapter. I'll wait. Hermione is about to punch Draco, finally. It's my favorite scene. Okay, you're back. A lot, right? You'll have to tell me how many; I didn't count. Millions of people with disabilities need IDs to work because we're not giving 72 percent of them SSI, we're not making the world accessible to them, and we're certainly not going to listen to them. But we absolutely should.

When Los Angeles County officials were reforming the county's elections system, they investigated how to make the best possible voting machines. They wanted them to be safe, easy to use, and easy to understand. As they researched, they realized that if they made all of the voting machines fully accessible, then not only would people with disabilities be able to vote at any machine and not just the crappy broken one in the corner that we see in most polling places, but voting would also be easier for *everyone*. Because the truth is, as much as ableism hurts people with disabilities—and that should absolutely be the priority, as is the case with all forms of isms—we are also hurting ourselves. Making the world accessible to all makes the world better for all. Mail-in voting was initially designed for people who couldn't leave their houses, and look at us now! Voting without pants in a variety of states! Imagine if the DMV was set up to be easily navigated by the person who has the biggest challenges getting around. What a glorious day in the park it would be for all of us. What if we thought of the idea of giving IDs to every American as an accessibility issue? What if we thought of everything as an accessibility issue? How much better would this world be for everyone in it?

The only other group of people whom we purposefully, forcefully, and systematically trap in government-mandated poverty like this are Indigenous Americans. I may be Black and female, but I am not sentenced to death if my grandmother sends me a birthday check. It doesn't have to be this way. I talk a lot about astronauts—as we all should. They are the world's greatest humans after grandmothers. One of my favorite podcasts, *Radiolab*, once did an episode called "The Right Stuff." It's about this incredible group of scientists, adventurers, and dreamers who all believe that their disabilities don't disqualify them from being astronauts. They believe their disabilities instead make them the strongest possible candidates, and that the modifications they make to the tools of space travel would make space exploration better for all of us. That episode, and those incredibly brave humans, blew my mind. They made me realize that getting every single American an ID is about more than just a job or shelter. For so many, it is the key to breaking free of a system that refuses to let them dream, to help them become the extraordinary humans that they are meant to be.

Takeaways:

1. The disability community is one of the most unseen but attacked and disadvantaged in America.

2. People with disabilities are more likely not to have IDs.

3. Accessibility benefits everyone.

9

No One Has Ever Really Pulled Themselves Up by Their Bootstraps

The good we secure for ourselves is precarious and uncertain . . . until it is secured for all of us and incorporated into our common life.

—Jane Addams, "The Subjective Necessity of Social Settlements"

H ello, this is Project ID."

"Oh my gosh, I'm so glad I reached you. You help people get IDs, right?"

"We do! Do you need one?"

"Not me, but I'm a caseworker, and I have several clients who have opportunities for housing but don't have an ID or birth certificate. Can you help?"

We get this call every single day for clients like Danny. Danny was homeless for ten years. He finally had an opportunity for housing, but one thing was stopping him: an ID. Government-issued photo identification is required to access almost all free or subsidized housing. Without it, you're stuck on the streets. The heroic case managers and social workers who work with the un-housed spend hours and hours trying to secure housing for their clients, but they almost never have the funds or capacity to get the IDs their clients need, and often are not trained in how to obtain out-of-state birth certificates or specialized documents to secure these IDs. So these workers do their best and seek out the resources they need to secure the services their clients need, but they are frequently stymied when the services become available and the client has no ID.

There is an assumption in this country that we have provided a large—some would say too large—social safety net for people who need an extra hand, so there is no excuse to be hungry, homeless, or unemployed. I had deluded myself into thinking that surely Americans had figured out that this wasn't even remotely the case, but then we gave people a little bit of extra money during the pandemic, and actual real-life senators felt okay saying out loud that people were probably spending that money on drugs. And I realized that maybe we still have some work to do.

The social "safety net" that we provide is small, shrinking, and inadequate. But when you have absolutely nothing, it's a hand up. So when you are unhoused or a returning citizen, or you have a disability or are trying to raise children in a car—or, as is very often true, you are all of the above plus a few—it can be a literal matter of life or death to have the opportunity to access subsidized housing; SNAP benefits (that's the Supplemental Nutrition Assistance Program, which you once knew as food stamps); unemployment, Social Security, or disability benefits; Temporary Assistance for Needy Families (TANF—emergency money for families with children); WIC (the Special Supplemental Nutrition Program for Women, Infants, and Children—supplemental nutrition and health-care referrals for low-income pregnant, breastfeeding, and postpartum women and children and infants under five years old); and Medicaid or Medicare. These programs determine whether you'll have a roof over your head, whether your children can eat, whether your baby will be born healthy, whether you can get health care. These programs are the key to survival for millions and millions of Americans. You may never have had to collect unemployment or feed your baby with formula you bought with a voucher, but you know someone who has—even if you don't know you do. In a country where the average resident doesn't have four hundred dollars to cover an emergency, these safety net programs have made the difference for far more of your neighbors than you think.

I often think about how lucky I am that my parents divorced in the 1990s. My mother hadn't worked in a while because she was a pre-internet military wife, but she was college-educated, and when she needed to find a job, the economy was doing well. She found a great job with a great company quickly, and we had a home and health insurance and occasional free tickets to the ballet until I graduated from college. It wasn't easy, and my mother, like all single mothers, is a hero for somehow surviving. I have one dog and a succulent, and honestly, the dog wouldn't be alive without my mother—and the succulent always has one foot in the grave. I cannot understand how my mother had a fifteen- and thirteen-year-old at the age I am now, and somehow we ate food every day and had running water. A lot of that is down to her, but we were also so incredibly lucky that she didn't need a job in, say, 2008. Or during a pandemic. What would have happened to us then? Would we have been living in a bright-green Chevy Cavalier? Would we have had to crowd in with my grandmother? Would we have ended up with no home, our belongings and IDs lost or stolen or confiscated by the police? The truth is, if we hadn't been lucky enough to live in a time when everyone was hiring, our lives could have gone a very different way. And it wouldn't have mattered that my mother had a great education and was a hard worker. If no one is hiring, no one is hiring.

Our client Rhonda was not so lucky. A single mother of two boys, Rhonda was doing everything she could to get her boys into safe housing after the pandemic. The apartment they'd had before she met us was so full of rodents that she had to leave, and now they had nowhere to go. Miraculously, her Section 8 certification—the US Department of Housing and Urban Development housing assistance program—came through, a doorway to a safe home. But you need an ID to claim your Section 8 housing, and she didn't have one. Through sheer luck, she found us, and we helped her get the ID she needed to move her children into a safe, rodent-free home. But it shouldn't be this way. I cannot tell you how often we get phone calls from *government public housing authorities* asking if we can get IDs for people they would like to place into housing. That is not a joke. If the government is providing services, they should make sure that the people who need those services have the documentation they require. This is, after all, government documentation needed for a government ID to access government services. And it's not just in order to *get* benefits, but also to *keep* them.

We have frequently had to help clients like Angie, in Georgia, who was about to lose her benefits because she no longer had a valid ID. The agency called us, and we were able to get her a new ID before they cut her off, a situation that never should have arisen. The same thing happened with Kate, who lived on her Social Security benefits, like so many of our grandparents. The thing about Social Security is that we all pay into it for our entire lives, and yet it's easy for the government to refuse to grant these benefits to us when we need them. Kate needed to reapply for her benefits—which is a thing they make you do— but her Social Security card was rejected because it was too old and weathered. Because, you know, you get one when you're born and then you're supposed to hang on to this unlaminated paper "card" for the rest of your life and keep it in pristine condition. When Kate went to the Social Security Administration to get a new card, she was told she needed a valid ID, which she didn't have. Kate depends on those benefits and didn't know how to find the $33.20 that she needed to get a new ID. We helped her, but again, we should not have had to. What is the point of offering services to people but not making sure that they can actually receive and retain those services? Unless, of course, that is the point.

I often think about how absurd it is that people's lives are changed because they happen to be lucky enough to run into a small organization started and run by a girl in her bedroom. Think about that. More than twenty-six million American adults do not have the photo ID they need for jobs, housing, food, medical care, and more. There are very few organizations to help them; the caseworkers, social workers, and agencies staffed with dedicated individuals whose job it is to help do not have the funds or ability to get people IDs. And admitting you don't have ID can often result in arrest, detainment, or worse. So the only hope is that maybe you're lucky enough to have a friend or a resource coach or a shelter that might point you in the direction of our organization, if you happen to live in one of our states; or maybe you're lucky enough to live in one of the few towns with a local ID org, and maybe they'll help. Of course, some organizations say they'll help with IDs but then require you to pay for everything (not out of cruelty, but because of a lack of funds), so that's really no help if you have no money. One notable organization would help an individual get an ID only if they "accepted Jesus Christ into their hearts." Florida.

We have these safety net programs that are really not providing much safety to anyone, but they're better than nothing. We say that we want people to use them to get back on their feet. I don't know if this technically counts as pulling yourself up by your bootstraps, because that phrase doesn't mean anything, and not one single person in history has ever done that, but either way, these services exist for exactly the situation that most of our clients find themselves in. And yet, over and over, every single day, someone sits across from me at a table or I get a phone call or an email telling me, "This person has the opportunity for housing, or for food for their children, or health care for their baby. But they need an ID. Can you please help?" We can, but we shouldn't have to.

You may be asking, "Why are you getting these calls from case managers and social workers? Can't they do this themselves?" Let me tell you, there is no more underappreciated American worker than the astronaut, but case managers and social workers are a close second. You may think we appreciate astronauts quite a lot, but we can never appreciate them enough. Case managers and social workers, however, get very little recognition for the work they do, and not nearly enough pay. I would also argue that astronauts do not get paid enough, but I guess getting to go to space is payment in itself. Back to the selfless servants who are case managers and social workers.

I should explain the difference. Social workers provide care and therapy to clients, while case managers help coordinate clients' treatment programs. Case managers help coordinate resources and agencies, while social workers provide critical emotional support and education. At Project ID, we mostly hear from case managers, but the reality is that the vast majority of care and treatment programs are understaffed and underfunded, and everyone does a bit of everything. That's why we hear from so many of these incredible humans. For brevity and because the majority of our partners are case managers, that's the job title I'll refer to from now on, but I did not want to leave out the incredible social workers who are so important for so many of our clients.

Most of the case managers we work with care deeply about their clients and their work. They would have to. You don't get into this incredibly challenging, emotionally taxing work for the money. Case managers are usually the people making sure that their clients are taking their medications, accessing health care and housing, finding job programs, and making sure they have all of their documents, including IDs. It's a lucky thing for a case manager not to be completely overwhelmed with more clients than they should be handling and not enough funding to adequately care for these clients. Case managers often have not had any training in how to get birth certificates—especially for clients who were born out of state—and IDs, and even if case managers have had training, they are almost never provided the funds for getting these documents and really don't have the time. But they also know that their clients need IDs to access most of the services the case managers are trying to provide for them. It's a rough catch-22. The other day I worked with a case manager with whom I have partnered often. She had another client who needed an ID. The client was born in Tennessee, so the CM not only did not know how to get the client's birth certificate but didn't have the $52.95 that it cost to get it. At Project ID, we have become experts at getting birth certificates without ID in every state, but that has taken years of research and hundreds of phone calls, and every day we are still figuring out new ways to make it happen. It took us about three years to figure out the best ways to get Social Security cards without ID, and that was before COVID hit and we had to learn all over again. Case managers are not document experts; when they come to us, it's because they need an expert to get the job done. We do train a lot of CMs to do this work, and many have gotten great at handling all but the toughest cases on their own, but many of our CM partners simply do not have the capacity to take this work on.

Once clients have the documents they need, in most areas they also need funds for IDs, which most case managers don't have in their budget. We solve this problem either by directly taking the client to the DMV and paying for the IDs or, more often, by giving the CM their own Project ID debit card so they can take their client at a time that works for them without having to coordinate through us. We always say that IDs are the key that unlocks the world of services, resources, and opportunities waiting for our clients. By working directly with case managers, we are able to get that key into a client's hands much more quickly.

None of us has accomplished anything alone, and the truth is that our clients often need more help than most to get on their feet. Our partnerships with case managers, social workers, other resource and support organizations, government agencies, and so many others are the only way that we are able to ensure that, once we get IDs into the hands of our clients, they are quickly able to use them to get what they need. It turns out that it takes a village to accomplish just about anything worthwhile.

Takeaways:

1. IDs are required to access social safety net programs.

2. The government requires government IDs to access government services but does not help the people who need those services get IDs.

3. Case managers and social workers are overworked and underresourced and often cannot get IDs for their clients.

10

The One Where
We Talk About Voting

*When it comes to our democracy, and who we determine
to have the right to vote . . . patience is no virtue.*

—Karine Jean-Pierre, "The *Shelby* Ruling"

At this point, you may be thinking, "This seems really obvious, and clearly almost every other country in the world has figured this out. Why haven't we just created a national ID, or at least made sure every person in every state has one?" Well, we could ask the same kind of question about universal health care, Eurovision, and high-quality baked goods. If you talk to politicians of any party about people needing IDs for jobs and housing, all but the most devoted QAnon believers will agree that everyone really needs an ID. That's not enough for most politicians to, you know, do anything about it—but they have a hard time denying the importance of IDs when you break the problem down for them. Yet if you ask that same person, "Hey, how about a national ID or free state IDs for every adult in each state?" they will look at you like the Area 51 alien just landed on your head and started belting show tunes. Why? Cowardice is one reason. We are no longer the nation that chooses to go to the moon not because it is easy but because it is hard. We are the nation that seriously considers the opinions of voters who don't think the moon is real. Fearmongering is another reason. The comical idea that once we have a national ID, *that's* when the government will really start tracking our movements is still spouted by organizations across the political spectrum. Possibly because they haven't heard of Google, social media, the Internal Revenue Service, the Social Security Administration, or teenage girls with a smartphone and a crush. Personally, though, I think the biggest reason is the fear, confusion, and partisanship surrounding the big hairy issue that got me into this business in the first place: voter ID.

Voter ID laws. That's probably what brought a lot of you to this book in the first place. The first time most people, including me, started to think about IDs was when voter ID laws hit the news. I've already told you that voter ID laws are the reason I started my organization in the first place, before I had the epiphany that changed everything. But that doesn't mean that voter ID laws have gone away. In fact, they have gotten worse.

Let's start with what voter ID laws are, and what they very much are not. At their core, they are what they sound like: laws that require a voter to have ID in order to vote. If you have read every chapter of the book so far, your brain is probably already screaming, "THAT'S SO UNFAIR! WHAT ABOUT TERRY AND KENDRA? THEY DESERVE TO VOTE!" Because you already understand the thing that most Americans and both major political parties do not understand, but that the people who designed these laws understand very well: requiring an ID to vote locks the most vulnerable people in our country out of their constitutionally protected right to participate in our democracy. But let's dive deeper into the laws first.

If you're wondering why you didn't start hearing about voter ID laws until the past decade or so, it's because they didn't really exist before then. A few states had something like modern voter ID laws, and some were testing out the laws and testing the courts, but for the most part these laws hadn't really caught on. This is for a good reason—we had a little something called the Voting Rights Act of 1965. The VRA and the Civil Rights Act of 1964 were the crowning achievements of the Civil Rights Movement. You can spend a few minutes Googling the major provisions of the VRA; we are just going to talk about one—Section Five. Section Five of the Voting Rights Act created something called "preclearance," a concept that required all of the covered jurisdictions to seek permission from the federal government before they made any changes to the voting process. These states in their entirety were covered jurisdictions:

- Alabama
- Alaska
- Arizona
- Georgia
- Louisiana
- Mississippi
- South Carolina
- Texas
- Virginia

Also covered were parts of the following states:

- California
- Florida
- Michigan
- New York
- North Carolina
- South Dakota

All of these jurisdictions had a long enough history of entrenched discrimination in the voting process that Congress determined that they couldn't be left to their own devices when it came to managing elections. So if Monterey County, California, wanted to cut early voting days in the county, its representatives would have to go to the federal government first. The federal government would take a look and—once it became clear that the result of that change would be to significantly reduce Black voter turnout—tell the representatives of Monterey County to kindly go home and be quiet.

For almost fifty years, Section Five protected voters, and the Voting Rights Act exponentially increased the number of voters of color who successfully made it to the polls at every election. Everything was going so well. Enter the 2013 US Supreme Court decision in *Shelby County v. Holder*. The good folks of Shelby County, Alabama, didn't think that they needed to be under the jurisdiction of the federal government anymore because they didn't have a racist bone in their bodies and, besides, racism was clearly over. So they sued. Their suit made it to the US Supreme Court, and that supremest of supreme courts decided, "You know what, you're right, Alabama. You couldn't be racist if you tried, and besides *we have a Black president now*, and Black people are out here voting, like, a lot, so obviously they don't need the protections that made it possible for them to do all of that voting! Huzzah! We've done it! We've ended racism. Go off and make whatever voting laws you want. Yaay."

If you didn't go to law school (smart choice), you may never have read a Supreme Court opinion in your life, and therefore, before that fateful day in 2013, you might not have known that Ruth Bader Ginsburg was the baddest Supreme Court justice to ever Supreme. But you knew after. Because the Notorious

RBG wrote a dissent that made the world stand up and pay attention. Her classic line—"Throwing out preclearance when it has worked and is continuing to work to stop discriminatory changes is like throwing away your umbrella in a rainstorm because you are not getting wet"—will live in infamy (but the good kind), especially because it ended up being an absolutely flawless prediction of the future. Within literal hours (not an exaggeration) of the Supreme Court's decision eviscerating Section 5, one of the most important parts of the Voting Rights Act, Texas and Alabama began working on passing voter ID laws. We went from just a handful of states with voter ID laws in 2013, to twenty-one states with those laws on the day Donald Trump was elected president of the United States, and we now stand at well over thirty states. More than half the states now have laws that say that state residents who are among the twenty-six million eligible voters in America who do not have government-issued photo ID cannot vote. And it's not just those states. If I want to vote in my neighborhood council election in my beachside community in Los Angeles, I have to show ID. If the first time you ever vote is in person anywhere in the country, you have to show ID. In more and more states, you have to show ID to even register to vote—good luck if you are hoping to register to vote before the thirty-day deadline and then make it to the DMV to get your ID before the election. Before 2020, only a few states required ID to vote by mail, but then a lot of people voted by mail in 2020—like waayyyy more than ever had before—and the states realized that this was a disaster, especially because a lot of those voters were young and people of color, so all of a sudden you started having to use ID to vote by mail all over the country. But don't worry, the Supreme Court is fine with that. In fact, these days, the Supreme Court is cool with basically any discriminatory or racist voting provision that any state can think of. And the states are really pushing this privilege as far as they can.

But let's back up. I can already see the questions swirling around in your galaxy brain. Your first thought was probably, "There are a lot of types of IDs! I've heard people talk about being able to use a gun license but not a student ID to vote. What kinds of IDs are people allowed to vote with? Perhaps this is a loophole!" Excellent question. The types of IDs you are allowed to vote with varies by state. In some states, you can vote with a current DMV ID, a passport, a military ID, aaaannnddd . . . that's it. Oh, and a tribal ID, because a lot of states tried not to allow that, and even the courts most hostile to voting rights were like, "Yeah, guys, you have to let folks with tribal IDs vote." But don't worry, the states are still finding tons of ways to prevent Indigenous Americans from voting, so we're still on brand.

In some states you can vote with school IDs, work IDs, government employee IDs, or other forms of ID. The list expands and contracts depending on the state. The gun license thing is a false flag. It sounds very sexy in a sound bite, but you have to have a DMV ID to get a gun license, so if you have one, they know you have the other. It's not nearly as terrible as attention-grabbing politicians like to make it sound. I figured this out when I came up with the brilliant idea to go to Texas and get as many brown people gun licenses as I possibly could, and then I read the rules, quietly said, "Oh," and unpaused *Game of Thrones*. The student ID issue, however, is another matter entirely. In some states, you aren't allowed to vote with a student ID at all. In Wisconsin, students can vote with their IDs if they include a name, photo, signature, date of issuance, and expiration date no more than two years after the date of issuance. Of the thirteen four-year UW system schools, only four had student IDs that complied with these rules, so the entire UW system had to create separate student voter cards that do. Many of the non-UW system schools have not taken that step. The state of Georgia has an actual list on its DMV website of the schools whose student IDs can be used to vote. High schools? No. Public and technical colleges? Yes. Private schools, such as many of the absolutely massive and prestigious historically Black colleges and universities that Georgia is known for? Do you even have to ask?

The next question that has come up is "BuT wHaT aBoUt VoTeR fRaUd?" Fair question. Proponents of voter ID laws bring it up often enough. But it's not a question that I will spend a lot of time on. The fact is every single reputable study has shown that voter fraud is just not a thing. It happens at a rate of between 0.0003 and 0.0025 percent. Here's how you know that voter fraud is not the actual reason that people want voter ID laws (besides the many, many times they have said it out loud in public in front of cameras): there is a slightly (slightly) higher rate of voter fraud in absentee voting. This makes sense. It's a lot easier to cheat when you're voting by mail than when you're walking up to an in-person polling place and there's a nice grandmother sitting there looking at you. You can't lie to a grandma. So there is a higher rate of voter fraud in mail-in voting, and by "higher" I mean that you're still more likely to get struck by the proverbial lightning, but it's higher. Yet, until 2021, the vast majority of voter ID laws were targeted exclusively at in-person voting, not voting by mail. Because these laws are not about voter fraud. They never have been.

For those of you playing 3D chess, your next question is, "But isn't there, like, a poll tax amendment?" Why, yes—yes, there is. Good catch. Buy yourself a chocolate. We covered this a bit in chapter 2, but I'm going to review it again; chapter 2 was a long time ago. The Twenty-Fourth Amendment—which passed in 1964, in case there is even a little bit of confusion about where it came from—banned poll taxes in America forever. And as we have discussed ad nauseam for nigh on thirty thousand words, IDs ain't free. So how do states get away with passing voter ID laws? Well, in some states, it's because they offer this little thing called a "free voter ID." It is free and would certainly allow voters to vote. These things are true. However, depending on the state, these IDs are almost impossible to get. In Georgia, they require almost as much paperwork as a DMV ID does. Also, no one knows they exist, and usually the educational budgets that accompany the creation of these new IDs are enough for a few cups of coffee and a box of off-brand donuts. Then, of course, there is the problem that we ran into from day one. Free voter IDs only allow you to vote, and for the vast majority of people who need IDs, voting is just never going to take priority over having a safe place to sleep at night and a way to feed their families. When you look up the charts of how many people are actually getting these free IDs, the numbers are laughable. You'll see a lot of zeros and almost never any double digits.

Beyond the free IDs, the argument is usually just "don't call this a poll tax, that makes us sound racist." The fact is, voter ID laws have been almost unbeatable in the courts, one of the many consequences of a decades-long conservative strategic process of moving the judicial system further to the right. It doesn't help that neither major party really cares about poor people voting all that much. That's why in 2021, when Democrats were pretending to try to pass a new Voting Rights Act, they immediately capitulated to Joe Manchin's plan not only to not eliminate voter ID laws, but instead to expand them to all fifty states. Everyone went on TV to talk about how much they suddenly loved voter ID laws and how we should definitely have them everywhere, and besides, it's fine because people can vote with a utility bill. Even Stacey Abrams and Barack Obama advocated in favor of Manchin's bill. Except tents don't have electricity, and homeless shelters don't hand out water bills. But the ID-less population is ignored, forgotten, and uncared for by everyone. We have a caste system in this country, and if you don't have an ID, you're an untouchable.

Takeaways:

1. Voting rights have taken a severe beating in this country over the past decade, and voter ID laws have been a big part of that.

2. Voter ID laws mandate certain types of IDs to vote; what those types are varies by state.

3. Voter ID laws are a poll tax that we don't call a poll tax. But that's what they are.

11

Give Me Your Tired

no one leaves home unless
home is the mouth of a shark

—Warsan Shire, "Home"

Have you ever been to a citizenship ceremony? It's incredible: a room full of people who worked so hard to come to this country (though many of us may wonder, "Why? Have you never heard of Sweden?"), determined to try their best to achieve THE AMERICAN DREAM™. They don't know yet that there is no American dream. They don't know yet that a full third of American adults believe in the shocking and wildly racist "replacement theory" and will try to kill them at the grocery store. They don't know yet that most Americans are just trying to survive.

No, at this moment these immigrants are happy, hopeful, excited new citizens. They studied for a test most people born in this country couldn't pass, paid the fees, waited years and years and years, and finally they're here. They get their Certificates of Naturalization, swear an oath, watch a recorded message from the current president, and walk into the sunshine as Americans. If America is great at anything, it's marketing, and Hollywood and Texas have really helped fuel a myth that has changed the world, and millions of people's lives, many times over. For a few wonderful, inspirational moments, these people are living that myth.

When, inevitably, some of those new citizens lose their Certificates of Naturalization, for one of the many reasons that we all lose documents, they will have to go through an extremely challenging process with US Citizenship and Immigration Services (USCIS) to replace it, including either paying $555 for a replacement document or applying for a fee waiver and then waiting months and months to be rejected, just as likely as not. In the meantime, if these people need a job or an ID, they are out of luck. When Amber's wallet was stolen, her Permanent Resident Card was suddenly gone. She was unhoused and trying to get on her feet, and suddenly her major lifeline was taken from her, and she absolutely did not have the $555 to replace it. She also wasn't even sure how to do so, the process was so complicated. Our volunteers were able to help her get her card replaced and get her to a DMV for the state ID that she also needed so that she could finally just focus on finding a home and starting her new life in America. When almost 40 percent of Americans can't come up with four hundred dollars in cash in an emergency, how do we expect people who are new to this country to some-how find the hundreds of dollars that it costs to replace their most valuable documents?

What if you haven't been lucky enough to make it through the citizenship process? It takes at least five years and a lot of money, time, and patience to be one of the lucky few who win that partic-ular lottery. Watching my stepfather go through the process was infuriating, and he was lucky enough to be married to an Amer-ican! No, they were not on *90 Day Fiancé*—I know you were wondering. We are not going to get into an immigration debate here, because the fact is, documented and undocumented immi-grants are here, whether you like it or not. And as members of our community who are driving on the roads and breathing the air and drinking the water, we have to take them into consideration when we are, say, crafting public health policy during a pandemic or deciding who does and does not get an ID in this country.

Only sixteen states as of this writing offer driver's licenses for undocumented immigrants. These licenses, called AB 60 li-censes, are obtainable without a Social Security number, but they still require quite a lot of documentation, which most undocu-mented persons do not have. But, most important, in many of those states you can get only a driver's license if you are undoc-umented, not an ID. Which means you have to be able to pass a written and driving exam, and you must provide a car for that driving test—with insurance. High on the list of things undoc-umented persons often do not have is a car and valid car insur-ance. At least five times a week, someone comes to me for help with an ID, and after deducing that they are undocumented, I have to tell them that I cannot help them unless they are able to pass two exams and provide an automobile. Why this discrepancy? Common belief is that it's easier to convince legislators that people need driver's licenses as a matter of public safety. If they just need IDs so they can pull themselves up by their proverbial bootstraps? Too bad.

As added insult to injury, in some states the words "not valid ID" or a literal black line are printed on AB 60 licenses just to be sure no one tries to vote or, heaven forbid, to get government benefits with one of these licenses. In some states, they make you prove that you've paid state taxes for the past two years (undocumented immigrants, by the way, pay billions of dollars in taxes every year). Reading the list of requirements to get an AB 60 license is like watching a Monty Python sketch. You see it right before your eyes, and yet you can't believe someone actually has the balls to do this. And this is in the states that are the *friendliest* to documented and undocumented immigrants. I keep coming back to the realization that we would not have this massive ID crisis if we just saw people as people.

In between citizenship and undocumented status lie a billion different states of legal being. The person next to you in a restaurant or the elevator at work could have one of many different types of cards in their wallet—from a green card to a work visa—and all of them have different requirements for reporting, eligibility, and security. Castello in Miami was here on a legal visa that required him to reapply every year. When Hurricane Andrew hit, he lost everything. Suddenly, he didn't have the documents he needed to reapply for his visa or get a new ID to find new stable housing, and a man who had been working hard to set himself up with a new life in America was suddenly homeless, jobless, and lost. Hurricane Andrew was in 1992. Castello didn't get a new ID until he found Project ID in 2021. In Virginia, Marco had been granted asylum and employment authorization, but while unhoused he lost his I-94 (asylum document), which the DMV required to get an ID. We were able to help him go through the USCIS process to replace the I-94, and that, along with the employment authorization, was sent to the capital for review before the DMV would finally give Marco an ID. What did Marco do when he had an ID? He immediately applied to join the National Guard. "To protect your home is the one thing I wanted to do, and the United States is my home," he said. This is a guy we want in this country. Why did we make it so hard for him to stay?

I do not believe that we live in a world where my dream of making sure that every single American has an ID will ever be extended to immigrants of any kind. I live here, I get it. But imagine how much more time, money, and attention we could give to all of these specialized cases if we reduced the number of people who needed to go to the DMV to get an ID by, say, the entire population of America over sixteen. Close your eyes and meditate with me. Envision a bright, sunny day. You drive to the DMV to take your motorcycle written test because you have decided to become a middle-aged baddie. You walk to the door. There's no line! You glide into an air-conditioned building, neat and clean and decorated for Star Wars Day because the DMV staff are so happy and have so much extra time on their hands. They're thrilled to see you. They smile as they lead you to the testing wing. You pass with flying colors. A beaming DMV employee takes your picture. As you leave, already planning your first moto road trip in your head, you see kind and patient DMV employees, no longer rushed and harried, slowly working through the ID process with a few families and individuals who look serious, but not scared, and grateful that they are being helped. You waltz into the parking lot and drive into the sunset. Life is beautiful.

You can open your eyes now. This is the world we can live in. We may not live to see my dream of being the first woman sent on a solo mission to Mars with nothing but a gin still and the complete works of P. G. Wodehouse, but this dream—the dream of a happier and friendlier DMV for all—is one we can achieve.

Takeaways:

1. Undocumented persons can get driver's licenses in only sixteen states and nondriving IDs in even fewer.

2. There are a wider variety of immigration statuses in this country than you think, and they all have different ID rules.

3. If every American had an ID, specialists would have more time to spend on the complicated immigration cases.

12

Pandemics Don't Care
About Your Gated Community

*Public health begins when all of us recognize the
humanity and dignity of every human being.*

—Bryan Stevenson

Common Situations for Which You Need an ID
(Incomplete):

- Get a job

- Adopt a pet

- Rent/drive/register a car

- Purchase tobacco products

- Open or access a bank account

- Purchase certain cold medicines

- Pick up certain prescription medications
- Purchase alcohol
- Apply for unemployment
- Purchase a gun or ammunition
- Purchase a cell phone
- Get a US Postal Service PO Box number
- Get a UPS Mailbox
- Visit people in many hospitals, particularly in pediatric units and maternity wards
- Pick up or send a package at FedEx or UPS
- Board a Greyhound bus
- Check into a hotel
- Enter government buildings
- Return an item for a refund at Home Depot
- Get a document notarized without witnesses
- Sign a lease or purchase a home
- Get married or file for divorce
- File a restraining order and other court documents
- Cash a check
- Enroll a child in school
- Take standardized tests such as the ACT, GED, LSAT
- Get toys from Toys for Tots

- Get a library card

- Access many food banks

- Stay at many homeless shelters

- Visit a new doctor or urgent care

- Apply for disability

- Donate blood or plasma

- Enter certain office buildings for job interviews

- Access WIC benefits for children

- Access food stamps or welfare

- Apply for a business license

- Get a government loan

The list is infinite. Can you think of any that I missed?

Be Identified at the Hospital If You're in a Coma

Catherine hadn't had an ID for eight years when she had a stroke. She arrived at the hospital in a coma, and with no ID in her bag, the hospital didn't have anyone to contact. Catherine's family didn't know where she was until she woke up. As soon as she heard about us, she got in touch; she never wanted to be stuck without an ID again. Thousands of John and Jane Does are checked into US hospitals every year. Some of them just didn't have their ID with them when they were injured. Many others don't have ID at all. Without being able to identify a patient, medical staff can't alert their families, can't look up their medical histories, and are taking huge risks when they treat patients they know nothing about. Our client Catherine was lucky that she woke up and found her family. For many patients, the ending is not as happy.

Get a COVID Vaccine or Test

When COVID hit, we all bought toilet paper, started making sourdough bread, and opened TikTok accounts. Then we got tested, constantly. The first thing I noticed when I signed up for my first test was that ID was required. We soon started getting reports about this across the country. As we were telling citizens of the world to stay home, wash our hands every five minutes, get our groceries delivered, and save the world by watching as much streaming television as possible, we were ignoring the fact that hundreds of thousands of Americans could not do any of those things. They were either crammed into shelters or living in tents on streets and in parks. They had no ability to wash their hands or bleach every surface on an almost constant basis. They also could not reliably find testing that did not require an ID they didn't have. And yet, COVID does not discriminate by class. Air molecules don't stop at gated communities. At the moment of the greatest public health crisis in a century, we finally remembered that we are living in a society, and the protection of one is the protection of all. Disease does not discriminate, even if we do.

Survive Major Changes in Public Policy

As I was writing this book, the US Supreme Court reversed *Roe v. Wade*, and life changed for a majority of Americans. Whether you stand on the side of women being able to make their own choices about their bodies or not, there is no denying that this decision will affect the health, wealth, and well-being of millions of women and children around the country. Seventy-five percent of women who get abortions in America are at or below the poverty line. In fact, not having the family income to afford another child is one of the top reasons that women choose to get an abortion. So, after reading those statistics and thinking about everything you have read in this book so far, your first thought was, I hope, "These are the same women who are far less likely to have IDs." Well done, both you and me. And yes, you are correct. Women living at or below the poverty line are of course less likely to have photo ID than middle- and upper-class women in this country. They are also the women most affected by this country's complete and total lack of accessible health care, our cruel insistence on not helping parents with childcare, and the continuing and worsening trend of housing costs outpacing wages so much that a person earning minimum wage has to work seventy-nine hours a week to afford a one-bedroom apartment in even an average housing market. Add the costs of health care, childcare, food, gas, clothes, and everything else it takes to raise a child, and it is no wonder that Project ID works with so many mothers and families who have been forced into homelessness because living in America is impossible for a huge percentage of our citizens. No wonder most women who seek abortions already have at least one child. They know how expensive it is to raise a child.

So, you may say, prevent the pregnancy before it even happens! Obviously, that would be ideal. But as a birth control baby whose brother is also a birth control baby, I can tell you for 100 percent sure that birth control is not a guarantee. You wouldn't be reading this book if it was! Even if it was, poor women often cannot afford contraceptives, especially if they live in the many states that did not expand Medicaid when they had the chance. One of the leading reasons that women seeking abortions say they got pregnant unexpectedly is that they either could not access or were not aware of their birth control options. If the next sentence out of your mouth is "Well, then don't have sex for pleasure," then this is not the book for you. We are helping people get IDs so that they can live the lives that *they* want to live, not the lives we want to impose on them.

So where do IDs fit into this? Well, you can already guess, especially if you have ever been to a doctor. You need an ID to access most types of prenatal health care. You need an ID to get most types of public or supported health insurance. You need ID to access preventive or emergency contraception in most states. You need ID to apply for WIC. And, more extremely, if you do have to fly out of state to access an abortion, you'll need ID at the airport too. So, whether you want to prevent abortions or provide better access to them, whether you are most concerned with a woman's health or her ability to care for the children she already has, women are going to need IDs.

Protect Public Health

The COVID pandemic was not the first time that rampant homelessness collided with a public health crisis, although before COVID we never really talked about it. Sometimes homelessness itself can cause a public health crisis. Right before the pandemic hit, Los Angeles was dealing with both typhoid and typhus outbreaks at the same time. While the majority of the cases were among the homeless, not all of them were. In fact, California's Governor Newsom was warning the state about this looming public health crisis just a year before the pandemic forced everyone to stay home, thus helping us avoid a potential major outbreak of these sixteenth-century diseases among the fortunate Angelenos who could afford to lockdown in their homes rather than sleeping on the streets. Homclessness may be more widespread in California than in other states, because California is by far the most populous state in the union, but cities across Texas, Washington, New Mexico, New York, Ohio, Kentucky, and more have all seen outbreaks of medieval diseases.

When we talk about IDs for life, this is what we're talking about. We're talking about a small piece of plastic that gives people the power to use the restroom indoors and take a shower every day. We're talking about a tiny card that gives human beings access to basic human rights like the ability to work a job that pays for healthy food and basic hygienic tools. When our clients say "I'm a person again" when they get an ID, this is what they mean. People experiencing homelessness die an average of seventeen years earlier than the general population. I spend a lot of time in tent cities and shelters across the country, and the conditions that human beings in the wealthiest nation of the world are living in are degrading at best and serious violations of their humanity at worst. But when we drive by the homeless woman and her children with a cardboard sign, or walk quickly past the tents on the sidewalk, or casually donate to a food bank without wondering why it exists in the first place, we're not seeing how much each of those lives affects ours. Not everyone who has been infected with typhoid has been unhoused. Of course not. We all breathe the same air and walk on the same streets. Even if we won't change policy to address issues that affect other people, after the pandemic, it is impossible to continue to close our eyes to the impact that our neighbor's health has on our own.

Let's look at public health another way. People experiencing homelessness have extremely high rates of alcohol and drug addiction and mental illness. Many people become homeless because of these challenges, but for those who become homeless without any of these issues, it is difficult to stay away from them for long. The realities of chronic homelessness are that encounters with drugs, alcohol, violence, and trauma are almost a guarantee, and the human psyche isn't built to endure those stresses for very long, so it's no surprise that 43 percent of America's homeless population has PTSD. When you're unhoused, every day is a struggle for food, safe shelter, and health care. There is also a lot of boredom. A lot of being homeless involves just sitting around. There are no meetings to attend, no parties to plan, no girls' trips or Netflix binges. So many of our clients talk about how there is nothing to do, but at the same time it takes much longer to do things. Long routes on public transportation to get to a clinic or a food bank, long lines at those food banks or soup kitchens to eat a meal. Long waits at shelters to get a bed, and then long hours following the shelter rules, which can include everything from a curfew to work shifts to mandatory hours in church. And then . . . nothing again. And all of this against a backdrop of increasing hopelessness for any kind of real future. I so often speak to clients who have been on the streets for decades and don't really believe that anything good can happen to them. I can see that even when I am ordering their birth certificates they don't really believe it will come, and for good reason. Vulnerable people are lied to and taken advantage of every day by the organizations and agencies that say they are there to serve them. So when their eyes fill with tears when I put their birth certificates in their hands, I get it. When they ask over and over, "But how am I going to pay for an ID?" and each time I respond, "We'll pay for it," I get it. I understand the fear and wariness and inability to believe. Well, that's not true. I don't understand; I couldn't possibly. But I get it. And I get why, when they get an ID in their hands, they so often say that their outlook has changed and that they believe now that there is a way out, and up.

But I digress. We're talking about how this affects you and

me. So, we have somewhere between half a million and three million (depending on whom you believe) stressed, traumatized, and possibly addicted unhoused human beings on the streets in this country. And then we have a nation that has chosen to criminalize homelessness, because this is a country where you have to earn the right to live, and damn you if you're not doing it the way we think you should. We talked about the revolving door earlier. Perhaps you're unhoused and sleeping on a bench or maybe, God forbid, you stole some food. So you're arrested and jailed. And then you are released, this time with a fine that you cannot afford to pay. You have no identifying documents, and now you have a conviction on your record, so good luck getting a job. So then you're homeless again. And then maybe you start doing drugs to cope with your PTSD, and then you're arrested, again. And so on and so on. Maybe it starts the other way, as it so often does. A youthful mistake lands you in jail, especially if you are Black or brown. You're released, but with no real way to get a job and maybe no home—or no healthy home—to go back to. So now you're homeless. Same problems. Same cycle. I cannot tell you how many men and women I know who have been stuck in this endless loop. As for the rest of us? Well, now we're dealing with high rates of recidivism, the incredibly high costs of both homelessness and incarceration, the continued trauma of homelessness in our cities, and—oh yeah—the massive crisis of medieval diseases permeating our air.

You'll note the one thing I have not listed yet: crime rates. I haven't done so because the research is extremely mixed and so steeped in assumptions and biases (on both sides) that, honestly, I do not believe that we have an accurate view of the correlation between homelessness and actual crime (I do not count sleeping on a sidewalk or loitering in a park as crime). What I do know is that, yes, there is most certainly crime committed by people experiencing homelessness, just as crimes are committed by many, many people who have homes. I do not think, for instance, that a single mass shooter or serial killer in America has been unhoused. But in a world of desperation, addiction, trauma, and fear, there absolutely will be crime. There is also a high and increasing rate of crime *against* the unhoused. Homeless women face significant sexual violence, and not just from homeless men. There are increasing reports of taser attacks on and thefts from the homeless (remember Ted?). In some major cities, there are increasing cases of homeless-targeted murders and assaults, as well as state-sanctioned crimes against the unhoused such as police sweeps in which authorities trash or even burn the belongings of the unhoused sleeping on public property. So, is crime committed by the homeless? Yes. Are they committing crimes at a higher rate than people who have a roof over their heads? I doubt it. Are they also significant victims of crimes committed by other unhoused people, by housed individuals, and by the system? They sure are. And none of that is good for any of us.

So, you may ask, what's the solution? Well, the most obvious is housing. Housing is health care, after all, and it is the only solution to homelessness. That may sound obvious, but pay attention to politicians for five minutes and you'll realize that housing is the last thing anyone is talking about. But that's what the obvious solution is. Even if we lived in a country where everyone had adequate health care, without homes we would still have millions of people living on the streets or crowded into shelters, where diseases, crime, and violence are all but guaranteed and where the costs for the general public both in actual dollars and in health and safety will remain untenable. Even now, when an unhoused person does get medical treatment or rehabilitation, after they are released they go back onto the street, where the problem starts all over again. The answer is housing, period. We need to build more, we need to make it affordable, and we need it now. Oh, and to get into that housing, do you know what every unhoused person will need? That's right: an ID.

Takeaways:

1. IDs are needed to do most normal things in life.
2. The economy, public safety, and public health are impacted by the ID crisis.
3. Individual health, wellness, and life are impacted by access to IDs.

Conclusion

Let us go forth to lead the land we love.

—JFK

Here we are, at the end. You made it! Congrats! You have learned several hours of selfless streaming bingeing and a serious brag post on Litsy. Thanks for hanging in there. I'm no Beverly Cleary, but I did my best. My greatest hope is that when you close this book, you'll take away three things:

1. That little ID in your pocket is life-changing for a lot of people and really hard to get. The story of [*insert name of your favorite client here*] really hit you in the gut, and you really need to tweet about them and tell all of your group chats.

2. We already have most of the tools in place to solve this problem, and it won't even cost that much; we just need the will to do it.

3. Always bring a book along when you go to the DMV.

If you remember those three points, I will have done my job. I wrote this book because I spend every day shouting as loudly as I can that there is a serious identity crisis in America; that we are never going to reduce our numbers of unhoused persons until we solve this crisis; that we are costing ourselves billions of dollars by forcing people to stay unemployed and unhoused rather than giving them a small plastic card that would enable them to get jobs and homes, to stay out of jail, and to take care of their families—and that solving this crisis is easy and cheap! Shouting isn't working, so maybe this book will. People take books seriously.

To underscore my point, let's talk about Honduras. Have you been? I have not, but I hear it's lovely. Honduras is a small country in Central America. Its population is roughly equal to that of Los Angeles County. Its nominal gross domestic product is about $16 billion less than Los Angeles County's annual budget. In 2020, Honduras faced not only COVID but also two (*two!*) tropical storms. Do you know what else happened in Honduras in 2020? The Honduran authorities biometrically registered and provided an ID for five million citizens—about 96 percent of the adult population—in six months. In six months, Honduras created a National Identification System that left no adult behind. Field staff traveled by car, bus, air, train, mule, and boat. They made sure that the process was inclusive of all demographics, especially the Indigenous populations and disabled and LGBTQIA+ communities. And they did all that while protecting their staff and citizens from a pandemic raging across the world. I have never been more impressed than I was when I read this story. I was also incredibly disheartened. My first thought was, "America will never do this." But then I remembered the history of this country. I remembered that when we started out, only a few white men with land had any rights, but now it's 2022 and I am a Black woman who has the right to spend all day watching Netflix and eating burritos if my heart desires. Progress.

The truth is, we can still do big things. We ended slavery and won votes for women and passed the Civil Rights Act and won the right to marriage equality. America is a lot of things, but one thing Americans are more than anything is a people who love to fight for something. It's kind of our brand. Good or bad, we're in the streets and writing letters and voting angrily. We love a fight, and we're great at it. Right now we are a broken nation and a divided people. Everything is terrible. Everything is going badly. Except national parks. National parks are a treasure and the only thing we are doing right in this country, and everyone should go thank a park ranger. They're right up there with astronauts. But other than national parks, things are pretty bad. And a lot of our problems, such as climate change and public education and Congress's refusal to implement term limits, seem like problems we can never change. They are so big and so out of our control and really frustrating and scary and terrible. I really enjoy water, and I live in California, so that's a real problem. It is also not a problem that I can solve. But this one is.

• • •

We can solve the identity crisis in America.

I believe we can, and we will, but I need your help. Right now, a bill sits in Congress: the IDs for an Inclusive Democracy Act, sponsored by Representatives Sean Casten of Illinois and Cori Bush of Missouri. Project ID Action Fund helped create this revolutionary bill, which would establish *a free federal ID for all Americans*. This bill would eliminate virtually all of the challenges that we have discussed in this book. If the Act is passed, our post offices, libraries, and social spaces would be the channels through which all Americans can obtain ID. The Act would give identity, and voice, to the more than twenty-six million Americans for whom obtaining a state ID has proved virtually impossible. The Act would even pay for and provide assistance with acquiring the documents required to get this ID. The free federal ID would be safe, secure, and usable in almost every way that a non–REAL ID state ID is usable. That would finally put us on the same plane as almost every other nation in the world. The Act would ensure that tens of millions of Americans could obtain jobs, housing, medical care—everything that you have read about so far. This bill would change everything, if it is passed. And we can pass it. We *will* pass it. But we need your help. Call, text, email, or visit your members of Congress. Visit idforid.org to find out how. Tell your friends and family. Post to social media. Tell everyone you know that there is a way, a simple, safe, cost-effective way to help twenty-six million Americans become part of society again. Tell them what you learned in this book, and ask them to take action. Together, we can do this one very, very big thing. Everyone on every side of the aisle can agree that giving every American an ID would decrease homelessness, increase employment, reduce recidivism, and—sure, why not—increase election security. These are things we all want. This is the big win that we can all achieve together.

So what do you do? You know I love assigning homework. Here goes:

1. I need you to share this book with as many people as possible. This is not a bid for royalties. The book you are holding in your hands may be the only book about IDs ever written, and if you have gotten this far, I hope you agree that these stories might help bring the issue to life for more people. We need as many Americans as possible to really understand this crisis.

2. Visit idforid.org for instructions on how to contact your members of Congress, scripts, social media posts, sample emails, book club guides, and much more. Beg, plead, and cajole your members of Congress into supporting the IDs for an Inclusive Democracy Act, and if they already do—a list is on our site—thank them!! Tell them how much you admire their courage and that they will be rewarded at the polls.

At Project ID, our number-one goal is to make sure that every single American has an ID. That's it. What they choose to do with it, whom they choose to vote for, how they choose to live their lives—all that is up to them, as it is for all of us. All we want to do, all we have to do, is make sure that every single American has the ID that will make it possible for them to embark on that glorious pursuit of happiness that we were all promised. We all deserve the same chance at life. Let's get to work.

Acknowledgments

I'll start with apologies to everyone I am going to forget. You'll know who you are by the end of this section.

Huge thanks to Monika Woods at Triangle House for being the type of agent who made me understand why people have agents. Thanks to Lauren for helping me find Monika.

Thanks to Patrik and the incredible team at Amistad and HarperCollins who made this book happen. I had no idea how many people it takes to publish a book and am truly in awe.

Thanks to all of the people I forced to read terrible drafts of my book and who sent perhaps more kind comments than I deserved.

Thanks to Meg and Russ for being sounding boards and complaints departments and sources of fun and inspiration and love and Harry Potter memes.

Thanks to Khaldon for being a great stepdad and providing me with the Marriott discounts that allowed me to write this book in silence without having to look at the chairdrobe piled behind me.

Thanks to my aunt Lynn for being the cool aunt who taught me about X-Men, and being a teacher, and taking the day off for birthdays and the premieres of new Batman movies, and helping with books and Vegas vacations when I was young(er) and broke(r).

Thanks to Daniel for offering both input and distraction and constant proof that his eleven-year-old son is smarter than I will ever be.

Thanks to Jenna and Emily and the entire Fireside team for being great publicists, but also just great people.

Thanks to everyone who works every single day helping the millions of ID-less Americans get the documents they need to live full lives, including Rick Mitchell and Joel Weiss from Homeless ID Project in Phoenix, Thomas Anderson at Inner City Law Center in Los Angeles, and all of the social workers, case managers, service providers, and people with incredible hearts who dedicate themselves to this work.

Thanks to our extraordinary clients who are living lives of courage, grit, and perseverance in ways both big and small every single day.

Thanks to Rep. Sean Casten for having the vision to see that America needs a free Federal ID and the courage to put his name behind our extraordinary bill. Thanks to Meagan and Lucy for working so hard to help usher that bill through the many barriers to success. Thanks to Rep. Cori Bush and all of the other members of Congress who have joined the fight, and to all of those who will.

Thanks to all of the volunteers who helped us get one ID or one hundred.

Thanks to the donors who are part of the small percentage of folks who will give to a Black-woman-led org and especially to that wonderful anonymous family foundation that has been with us since the very beginning and without whom I would have had to get a job at Starbucks.

Thanks to our incredible partners who spend their days and often nights and weekends working to make a change in a country that doesn't make it easy, including our long-time partners at Orleans Public Defenders led by the incredible Wan Qi Kong.

Thanks to Bill and Thierry and Salim for supporting me in the background from day zero and then stepping up to join the board when I really needed you.

Thanks to J. Kelly for being a friend and a mentor and general life goals.

ACKNOWLEDGMENTS

Thanks to Gayle for being a magical presence and helping me figure out where I go from here.

Thanks to Butch and Sundance and Drs. Grant, Saddler, and Malcolm for keeping me going for the last thirty years or so.

Thanks to Earl Grey tea, the real MVP.

About the Author

Kat Calvin is the founder and executive director of Spread The Vote + Project ID and the cofounder and CEO of the Project ID Action Fund. A lawyer, activist, and social entrepreneur, Kat has built a national organization that helps Americans obtain the IDs they need for jobs, housing, and life, and that also allows them to go to the polls. She is working towards the passage of the IDs for an Inclusive Democracy Act and pro-ID legislation across the country.

Kat is an enthusiastic photographer, an avid traveler, a mildly obsessive reader, and a deeply passionate watcher of streaming television. Kat attended Mount Holyoke College and the University of Michigan Law School. She is an Army brat mostly from Seattle and Arizona, and currently lives in Los Angeles.